GLANCING ASKANCE

Even More Essays on

People and Food and Stuff

By

Marc Wollin

To Matt and Dave

Who have listened to my stories and

laughed at the right times.

Mostly.

GLANCING ASKANCE

Even More Essays on People and Food and Stuff

INTRODUCTION

Let me be very clear: I am no George Bernard Shaw. That Nobel Prize and Academy Award winning writer, known best for his plays such as "Man and Superman," "Candida" and "Pygmalion" was a literary giant whose work is still studied closely more than half a century after his death. His discourses, literary wit and prodigious output marked him by many as second only to Shakespeare among English writers. That brilliance is somewhat tempered by his controversial views on a number of topics, raging from his admiration for Mussolini and Stalin, and his opposition to vaccination and organized religion.

None of that is me. About the only place where a Venn diagram of the two us might cross is in an earlier period of his life wherein he was a weekly columnist for The Spectator in London. He wrote music and theatre reviews for several years, eventually giving it up to focus on playwriting. Asked why he stopped, he talked about the stress and commitment that was required. He likened writing a weekly column to standing under a windmill: you no sooner dodged one blade and straightened up, proud of yourself for the accomplishment, then another was angling directly for your head. You and me both, George, you and me both.

Still, I keep doing it because it has somehow become a part of me. This third collection is but a sample of the words from the more than 20 years I have been on this journey in the wilderness. No, they are not Shakespeare nor Shaw nor anything even close. But like the works of those giants, I recognize that it's a privilege to put one's thoughts together, and know that others are taking their precious time to digest it. It was the playwright Tom Stoppard who noted that words are innocent, neutral and precise... but "If you get the right ones in the right order, you can nudge the world a little." I'm not so self-assured to think I can move the entire planet, but if something I write gives a gentle prod to a reader or two, I'll allow myself a small smile.

People often ask me how I can pen a new essay every week, and indeed, I often wonder myself if I'm approaching the end of the line. After all, the easy and obvious ones were written long ago. Still, it's gotten so the effort to write each one is more or less like brushing your teeth: nothing will happen if I don't do it, and yet if I don't do it I feel as if I have forgotten to do something important. Added to that is that fact that the number of things that attract my attention is never ending. The trick is figuring out how to make it of interest to you. If there is an overarching goal to any of this, it is that: to share what interests me with you in a way that makes you want to pass it on.

On a shelf in my office I keep a series of notebooks with clippings of each of these efforts. Each time one appears, I scissor it out and slip it into a plastic sleeve. Each book is about an inch across, and holds about 26 double sided pages, which conveniently works out to 52 clippings, a year's worth of output. As I write this and look up, I currently find myself nearing the end of the 23rd black blinder in that series, and about to start the 24th. It's worth noting that by the time Shaw died, his collected works spanned 36 volumes.

George, I'm coming for you.

Marc Wollin

September 2018

PEOPLE

Trader Joe

(2014)

Alumni of Goldman Sachs have had to deal with a wide variety of issues in their next careers. There's the future of the banking system (former Secretary of the Treasury Henry Paulson) and the control of interest rates in Europe (President of the European Central Bank Mario Draghi). Others have had to grapple with the intrigues of the White House (former White House Chief of Staff Josh Bolton), as well as the running of the state of New Jersey (former Governor Jon Corzine). But probably not many have had to deal with the fact the stuffed clams have too many breadcrumbs. Then again, they're not Joe Mazzella.

Joe had a twenty year career trading commodities at the flagship Wall Street firm. But when his daughter had her sixteenth birthday, and introduced him at the candle lighting by saying "This is my dad, and I never get to see him," he knew it was time to leave. So he cashed in his chips, and started to trade for himself. Then one night his softball team stopped by a local watering hole 5 minutes from his house, a place that wasn't really making the grade. It turned out it was for sale, and Joe had always wanted to own a restaurant. He knew nothing about the business, but had a childhood friend who did, and who agreed to supply the knowhow if Joe supplied the cash. And before you could say truffle mac n' cheese, Somers 202 was born.

He figured it would be fun; after all, how hard could it be? You sell a steak for $10, you make $2, and you have a place that always has a table for you and your wife. "I was hoping to generate a little income, just pay the bills on the place," he told me. But he quickly found out that wasn't the case. "Because I live in this town, I had to throw that out the window. You can't cut corners. Every stoplight, every corner, I'm getting honked at. I can't go low end. Plus I eat here myself."

Joe wanted a place he could be proud of, one that had legs and built a following. But he's not a cook: "There's a swinging door into kitchen; when I go in, I'm a tourist." So he looked at the place the way a customer would. "People who come here know they're always going to see the owners. We don't tell people, but by the end of the night you know." Joe walks the room, checking on the tables, making sure everyone is happy. "There's an old Italian custom that you never come to visit empty handed. So I'm always giving out desserts." He laughs: "The staffs says 'You're the reason we're not making any money!'"

He also approaches it like a business, using some of the skills he gained on Wall Street. He still trades commodities, and if he sees a spike in the price of pork or beef or propane, he adjusts his restaurant purchases accordingly. He created two separate areas inside, a bar and a dining room that play to different crowds. He's very tied into the community, hosting gatherings of Girl Scouts and sports teams. And he notes that the restaurant business, like the financial world, is all about paying attention to the margins. "That's what makes the difference," he said. I asked for an example. "Take vodka. Most places will buy 4 or 6 bottles a week. We just bought 100 cases, and got a great price, like 60 cents on the dollar. In the long run, that will pay off."

Still, he acknowledges that to do it right is hard work. "It's much more stressful than trading commodities. It's an open mirror, a huge reflection of yourself, and that means you're obliged to do everything the right way." And he's not just sitting still. This year they added a deck, have plans to put in a raw bar for seafood, and he's excited about a deal he just struck with a local farm to use their produce. But even after a successful four years, he's going slowly; while he'd like to open another place, he doesn't want to sacrifice the quality and control he has at the one location. Still, for all the headaches, it does have its upside: "It really is a lot fun. And when people walk out with a smile, it really is worth it."

Sara's Smile

(2016)

I have seen the future, and its name is Sara.

The funny thing is I don't know all that much about her. We were in Stockholm, and taking a day trip to an outlying island in the archipelago. The capital of Sweden is made of 14 islands itself, connected by 57 bridges. But that's nothing compared with the dots of land sprinkling the sea on the city's east side. Exactly how many islands is debatable, with headcounts ranging from 14,000 to 100,000: the general consensus is around 24,000. But ask almost any Swede, and they will have their favorite and gush rhapsodically about it.

We were on our way to Utö, which sort of rhymes with "pewter." The island sports a hotel, a few restaurants, a mining museum, a bakery, a miniature golf course, a tennis court, and plenty of hiking and biking trails. But when we were there the first week of September, all but the hotel were already closed for the season. No matter: the trails were well marked, the view of the Baltic sea was breathtaking and the herring was delicious.

To get there requires a train/bus/ferry combo from the center of town. If you speak Swedish, it's likely not much harder than going to the Jersey shore from Manhattan. But at least for this English-speaker, the danger lay in spraining my tongue as I tried to confirm the directions with the ticket taker at the train station: "So I take the Nynäshamn train as far as Västerhaning, then catch the bus to Årsta brygga, where I get a Waxholmsbolaget ferry to Gruvbryggan. Right?" Go ahead: you try it.

We managed the first leg no problem, and were looking for the bus stop. On an hunch, we aimed for a spot where people were congregating. There were a bunch of young teenagers loaded with camping gear, and what turned out to be a club of pensioners on a day trip. I approached a woman in the second group, and asked if they were also headed to Utö. It took her a moment to decode my pronunciation, but then she smiled broadly, confirmed it and invited us to follow them.

While we waited we chatted with the pensioners about travel and such. When the bus came I chose a set of two seats facing two others, hoping some of our new acquaintances might join us. But down flopped 2 young girls, jabbering madly with their friends. They piled sleeping pads atop duffel bags, and settled in for the short ride to the ferry.

Turned out they were middle schoolers going on a field trip. Sweden is a very homogeneous country; most people walking down the street are blond and blue-eyed, and the locals we spoke to confirmed it as well. Diversity means people with long hair and short hair. In that light, both Sara D and her pal Sara H stood out not because they were wearing tie-dyed shirts that said "North Carolina," but because both were dark skinned with a mix of features.

Sara D was the chatty one. Her family was from Kurdistan. They had been in Sweden a year, and she loved it. She especially liked that girls were equal to boys. She spoke 5 or 6 languages (she wasn't sure if two dialects of Arabic counted as one or two). She said her old home was a difficult place in which to live, but she loved the freedoms and ease of her new one. And while she wasn't sure what she wanted to study later, she knew she wanted to be a boss. She told us about her studies, quizzed us about our trip, lighting up the entire time. Unfortunately, when I asked her, she also realized she had forgotten the marshmallows for that night.

We often say that with all the problems we have today, our best hope for the future lies in our children. They have a different world view than we do, one that looks past many of the divisions that separate us. When we say that, we usually think of our own kids; nothing wrong with that reference point. But now when I think of what's ahead, and the kind of person that will make a difference, my kids will be joined in my mind by another. For we can only hope that the future is also partly shaped by people like Sara D.

Live From Brooklyn

(2017)

Dave was filling the smoke machine, Tony was tweaking the lights and the band was sipping beers in the green room. They were going live in less than an hour, so that was all routine. But when the studio is one you built with your own hands in an old garage behind your parents' house, stuffed with $100,000 worth of gear and run as a passion project with the help of family and friends, things don't always go smoothly. The master computer was hung up and Katie had to reboot it, and they were calling one of the cameramen who lived down the block to "come over already." But at least the audio guy was just a few minutes away according to his GPS. Just one problem: he was pulling up to 78th Street in Queens when the studio was in Brooklyn.

None of this seemed to faze Paul Liatsis, the not-yet-30-year-old driving force behind Bridgeside. Paul had started his production company as a wrapper for his freelance work, tried producing his own comedies and even got his pilot "Work In Progress" about 2 slackers working different jobs accepted at a couple of film festivals. But coming from a family of musicians, and even playing in a band with siblings and cousins, it was only a matter of time before the cleaned-out garage became more than just a rehearsal space.

He had seen his sister ("The kid with the real talent!" he laughs) struggle as an actress and not get rolls, before giving up and turning full time to music, a profession where she called the shots. That led him to realize that whatever he did he wanted to make his own content and control it himself. And so while many dream of making a show or writing a song, Paul took the long view: he wanted to create a channel.

He had been living with his cousin, but with all the kids out of the house, his folks took the apartment on the second floor and Paul moved back in and claimed the first. And he started to upgrade the stage they had built in the garage to be more of a studio that could handle live shows. He added more lights and cameras, ran the wires underground to the house, turned the room behind the kitchen into a control room including a high-end audio system, and turned the mud room into a green room. "If I'm gonna live at home," he said, "I'm gonna have the best badass space I can have."

His sister's band was the guinea pig. Under the banner of Bridgeside Live, he recruited friends and family as crew, and went online with a live one-hour performance show. It was a disaster. The sound was bad, the sync was off. He felt horrible, but rather than be cowed he doubled down. He tweaked the equipment, added better gear where he could and started calling local bands with a free offer of airtime. In the beginning it was hard. But then word started to get around about the cool stage in Brooklyn, about the after-party screening in the tent with the fire pit, about the chance to be live on YouTube and Facebook where fans could watch.

Now after doing it weekly for a year, he's got a steady supply of talent filling up his regular Tuesday night 9PM slot. He's added a Q&A session with the band after a 50-minute performance, and edits the sets into individual songs he posts each day for the next week. The night I visited they smoothly showcased journeyman musician John Santiago and his current project of Johnny and the Bootlegs, jamming through nearly an hour of original material and registering over 500 views on Facebook Live. And anyone watching the 7-camera show could be forgiven for not knowing it was originating from a garage in a quiet residential part of Bay Ridge.

Paul and his gang have started to branch out into other genres. They produced a pre-Golden Globes show that focused on fashion, and have cooking and sports programs in the works. But what he's most excited about is the community he's building. "This isn't about me," he says, "it feels more like a movement." He laughs: "I don't want to go all Olive Garden on you, but when you're here, it feels like family."

End of Her Era

(2015)

Dear Susan;

For the last 12 years, you have skipped innumerable dinners with me. We have had a generous number of policy disagreements. I have fielded hundreds of "please can you take a look at this" requests. And more than a handful of times you have asked in your nicest voice if I would help draft (translation: write in its entirety) a speech, column or memo under your byline, though you were quick to give me ghostwriter credit (or so you said).

To truly balance the ledger, however, one needs to consider the context for those actions. In your roll over those same dozen years as a member of the Board of Education, and in the last 8 as its President and last 2 as the president of the county association, you have spent untold hours working so that the kids in our community get the best education possible. You have worked tirelessly to support the teachers, administrators and staff as they perform the Herculean task of refocusing their charges' attention from Facebook pages to textbook pages. You have talked with uncountable parents, far more unhappy than happy, usually with patience, but always with a genuine desire to help. You have earned the admiration, sometimes grudgingly so, from those who want nothing but the best for the schools, as well as those who wonder how we can continue to pay for such largesse. And you have shaken the hands of hundreds of graduating seniors, a task which brings the same smile to your face as when you don a tall red and white striped hat and read Dr. Seuss to kindergarteners.

Upon reflection, I'd say the scales balance nicely.

While it's usually credited to Mark Twain, it was his friend and collaborator Charles Dudley Warner who wrote "While everybody talks about the weather, nobody does anything about it." Public education is much the same. It's an easy whipping boy, a critical task requiring large amounts of capital with a million variables, many beyond the control of the people in charge. Why would anyone want to be involved in such a seemingly no-win endeavor? It all but defines the phrase "dammed if you do, dammed if you don't."

And yet you stepped up to the plate, and continued well after our kids had moved on. True, your reasons in the beginning were selfish: to try and have some say in the educational process that directly affected our boys. Still, it was a natural progression from your efforts as a class mom, to serving on various district committees, to finally standing for election. Add to that the fact that you were a graduate of the district, and the daughter of a teacher from the same, and it now seems in hindsight more inevitable than not.

Your first campaign brochure, which actually never actually got used, said it simply: "It's a tough balancing act. On the one hand, we all want the best educational system for our children. On the other, there are a limited amount of resources. Sometimes it means saying yes. Sometimes it means saying no. But now, more than ever, it will require school board members who are will ask tough questions, challenge conventional thinking, and look for ways to maximize the dollars we have available. I'll take that responsibility." You did, and you still do. (On a side note, the brochure also included space for hoped-for endorsements, including one I mocked up from your dad: "Vote for my daughter. I might.")

To be fair, not every decision you and your colleagues made worked out. But anyone who thinks that you didn't agonize over the choices, carefully weighed the options and chose the course you sincerely thought was the best would be sorely mistaken. Some might fault you for any number of things, but not caring and not trying to get it right can't possibly be among them.

And now it's time to move on. You indeed took that responsibility, but now it's someone else's chance. Whatever you next turn your attention to will be fortunate indeed to have your gaze upon it. On the occasion of moving to that next challenge, all who benefited from your tenure can only offer thanks for all you have done for all the kids, ours and others, past, present and future.

With admiration, congratulations and much love, your ghostwriter.

First Responder

(2016)

Quincy was up front about it. No "I wanted to help people." No "I couldn't wait to get out on my own." No "I really looked up to him and wanted to be like him." Yes, all have a kernel of truth to them. After all, he was a teenager with a neighbor who was a fire captain, and the sixth of eight siblings, so any of those rationales could have been ones as to why he wanted to be a volunteer fireman. But he's nothing if not honest. His reason for starting down the path he's on? "There were girls at the fire house, and I wanted to drive like a maniac." Worlds have been built on weaker stuff.

But that was how it started. He got his advanced training, worked as an EMT and continued with his local department. For sure there was driving fast and showing off for the ladies, but it had its much more difficult side as well. He recalled how in the early hours of a Sunday in 1996 he responded to a head-on collision. He climbed into a mangled car past one lifeless body, and helped pry a still breathing one from the back. He helped get that one to a chopper, but he also died from his injuries. It took several hours to clean it all up, and Quincy started home just as the sun was coming up. Though it had been a while since he had been in church, that morning he felt the need. He pulled into one near his house, sat in a corner pew and cried. He was just 18.

He dropped out of high school in his senior year, but kept home schooling to get his diploma. He worked a succession of jobs, including professional EMT and bartender. When his girlfriend dumped him via cell phone, he spent the night drinking, then drove the next morning to the Coast Guard recruiting office and asked how fast they could sign him up. After ascertaining that he wasn't wanted by the cops, the recruiter asked for the name of the girl and completed the paperwork. Two weeks later she called, and they got back together. The next day he left for boot camp.

His first post put him in the Caribbean looking for drugs and illegal aliens, as well as doing humanitarian work. "But I did learn to drive a boat fast, and got lots of sunburns." That girl turned into his wife, and with his first kid on the way, he transferred to a station on Staten Island. When his four-year hitch was up, he left to join the NYC Fire Department, and was assigned to Ladder 42 in the South Bronx, arguably one of the busiest and most dangerous posts in the city.

He kept his reserve status. "But let's be real, this was the CG we are talking about. How likely was it that I'd be recalled?" Likely, as it turns out. Three years later, in order to help prevent another attack like the one on the USS Cole, he was sent to the Middle East to do port security. A year later he was rotated back with a medal. Wanting to use all his skills, he was accepted as part of the FDNY Marine Division for their busy summer season. I asked him if the pressure ever gets to him. He laughed. "I have the best job in the world. Half the year I am assigned to the best ladder company in the FDNY, and half the year I get to drive a boat around New York City. So no, I don't want out."

For a guy whose day to day involves working in some of the toughest environments there are, he's relentlessly upbeat. "I don't do it for the thanks. I've established that I can get paid to do work that I enjoy that just so happens to be helping people." And when he gets tired of all that adrenaline rush, there's his other sideline: "I'm also an ordained minister, with 30+ ceremonies under my belt." I asked him what was the common thread of it all: "I just love seeing people happy."

Final tally: he loves what he does. He gets to help people. His girl is his wife. And he still gets to drive fast. As far as Quincy is concerned, that's a win-win-win-win.

Capturing Grace

(2012)

The "Five-Stage" model of grief by Elisabeth Kübler-Ross was first put forth in her 1969 book "On Death and Dying." And while it was meant to explain the feelings a person goes through at the end of life, it's since been adapted to divorce, substance abuse, even breaking up with a boyfriend. By now it's become so much a part of popular culture that there are five stages to everything from travel (dreaming, planning, booking, experiencing, sharing) to drunkenness (smart, handsome, rich, bulletproof, invisible).

Whatever the intent, the original five stages of denial, anger, bargaining, depression, and acceptance are also applicable to those with a major illness or injury. Be it cancer or a shattered leg, one can easily see the same progression play out as an individual comes to grips with their situation. It's especially true with slower, degenerative diseases such as arthritis or heart disease. But it's a fair bet that with all the permutations she might have considered, Kübler-Ross' didn't look at those with Parkinson's Disease and add a sixth stage of "dancing."

Yet, perhaps she should have. At least that's the conclusion one could draw from a remarkable program that originated at the

Mark Morris Dance Company in Brooklyn. Called "Dance for PD," it started in the fall of 2001, and has since expanded to 75 communities around the world, including those in New Zealand and Tel Aviv. In the same way that singing can help those that stutter, the movement and flexibility that is required in even simple dance seems to help those whose muscle control is slipping away.

It's more than just an idea. As David Leventhal, a former principle dancer with the Mark Morris company who now devotes all his time to the program says, "things like balance, movement sequencing, rhythm, spatial and aesthetic awareness, and dynamic coordination seem to address many of the things people with Parkinson's want to work on to maintain a sense of confidence and grace in their movements." However it's one thing to hear the theory; it's another to see it come alive. And that's where Dave Iverson comes in, and his remarkable film "Capturing Grace."

Iverson is an Emmy award winning writer/producer/director with credits a mile long for a variety of PBS shows such as Frontline. He stumbled upon the program while researching his acclaimed documentary "My Father, My Brother, and Me." That film examines Parkinson's through the very personal lens of his own family, where three members have been diagnosed with the disease. That's right: Dave has Parkinson's as well.

"Capturing Grace," as yet unfinished, chronicles the program and some of its participants as they prepare for their first public performance. We meet Joy Esterberg as she slides across the rehearsal space, ending with jazz hands: "You're feeling it, and doing it utterly to the sense you can imagine it, then you're there." Or Carol Eneski, whose body shakes when she talks, but whose arms trace graceful arcs when the music is playing: "I want us to be good. I don't just want us to be good for people with Parkinson's." And Reggie Butts, built like a linebacker, who had to stop attending class when he was admitted to the hospital for a time, eventually making a slow and deliberate yet triumphal return: "When the dance class is going on, there are no patients. There are dancers."

It is a remarkable portrait. To help finish it, Iverson has turned to Kickstarter.com. There you can watch a trailer, but more importantly, help: I and others have contributed funds towards production. Pledges of $5 receive a "Thank You" card from the filmmaking team featuring a photo by Director of Photography Eddie Maritz, while $500 or more garners a special preview along with dinner with Iverson and others involved. They are crossing their fingers: as of this writing, they are about halfway to their modest $15,000 goal with just a few weeks left, and Kickstarter is an all or nothing proposition.

Speaking for myself, I would encourage you to check it out and donate to the film if it moves you. Yes, my father had Parkinson's, as does my good friend Andy. But it's not about me or them or even Iverson. It's a story about people who have decided not to just roll over when hit by a disease that stops many in their tracks. Or as Mark Morris himself says, "The people who come in the building one way leave another way. And I don't mean by a different door. They are transformed."

Anthony

(2016)

As I finished tying my tie, I picked up my phone and texted a quick question to the crew: "You guys in?" Back came the answer. "Missing paperwork. Waiting for building clearance." I sighed. I was in a hotel room, having gotten 3 hours of sleep after flying in from the last gig. I had been hoping for a hassle free morning, but the best laid plans and all that.

I riffled through my bag to find copies of the paperwork. The location was only a few blocks away; I could be there in 10 minutes. But strike two: I had the forms on my laptop, but hadn't printed them out. Sigh again.

Still, not a major setback. As with most hotels, I assumed here would be a computer in the lobby. I copied the documents to my memory stick, and headed downstairs. No problem, the manager assured me. In the back of the breakfast area was a setup, and I was welcome to use it.

The lounge had a smattering of tourists and business people, and a number of different languages tumbled about. There was a long counter with cereal, muffins and fruit. Next to a toaster and microwave, a young man in a shirt and tie was helping people with the do-it-yourself waffle iron. And at the end of the room, my savior: a keyboard, screen and a beat-up printer.

I popped my stick into the computer and woke it up. I quickly pulled up the first document, and hit "print," waiting for the comforting hum of the printer going about its business. Nothing. I gave it a few more seconds, but it didn't come to life. I checked the computer and printer, but both seemed to be connected and functioning correctly. Strike three: the day was not getting off to a good start.

I went to the front desk, and explained the problem to the manger. He apologized, but before he could say anything else, the young man from the waffle iron stepped over. "C'mon, sir, I'll help you," he said with a smile. The manager smiled as well: "Not to worry sir. Anthony will get it going for you."

As we walked back into the lounge, Anthony greeted some newly arrived guests: "Good morning! Coffee's over there. Help yourself to anything. If you need help, I'll be right back." He then turned to me. "Sorry for the trouble, sir. I know my printer, and she's getting a little old. But don't worry, I know how to get her started." We walked over to the computer. He checked it as I had done: I tried all that, I said. He laughed: "Oh, so you know computers! Well, this one can be a little fussy. Just gotta show it some love, and she'll work." He opened the front panel and closed it. Then he gave it a little shake, and pressed the button on top. Sure enough, we heard a whir and my documents came tumbling out. I laughed as well and thanked him, as he went over to the help someone make waffles.

While the machine was printing, I got a cup of coffee and watched Anthony. He moved quickly from place to place, showing new guests where things were. He told an obvious boss about a table that was lopsided. When some people asked about the waffle iron, he explained it was for making "gofry." It looked it up later: Polish for waffles. Anthony's linguistic skills had their limits, however. The same folks brought a bottle over to him and asked him what it was. "Blueberry syrup" elicited blank stares. Not easily deterred, he quickly pulled out his phone, punched up Google Translate, and showed them the answer. They grinned broadly.

I stopped on the way out to tell the manager what a great employee they had in Anthony. As he wandered over as well, I told the manager how he not only helped me, but how much he was helping all the people in the back room. His boss smiled and agreed, but also admonished the guy that he had to get to work on time. Anthony grinned sheepishly, a detente of sorts. With that, I headed out. Of course, by the time I got there, the paperwork had been found. But printing it wasn't a total waste: it gave me a chance to meet Anthony.

Looking Good

(2014)

First she had to deal with a bunch of revolutionaries in tattered rags. Next it was a troupe of dancing Arabians in flowing robes. Then it was mobsters in fedoras and pinstriped suits. And that was just Sunday. Monday it was sportscasters describing hockey, while Tuesday meant a couple of business execs explaining earnings. But if you're Belinda, it's just your typical week, especially when you're the makeup artist that everybody wants.

True, not every week has her as the Department Head for the Tony Awards, the key makeup artist for the Stanley Cup Finals or working with the CEO of a major corporation. But if it's not one thing, it's another. It might be a music shoot in Nashville or a network singing competition at Radio City, a photography session for a print ad or even a wedding. No matter: whether it's Billy Graham or Billy Joel, George Clinton or Hillary Clinton (yes, she's done them all, plus McCartney, Sting and more), they trust her to make sure they look good.

Belinda began her working life as a model in her native Florida, and even managed two bars on the beach in St. Petersburg. "I made a lot of money!" she told me, but she didn't like the lifestyle. And so she made a promise that by the time she was 30 she would go on no more auditions and pour no more drinks (unless they were for herself). She enrolled in a vocational school for TV production, graduated when she was 31 and got work with ESPN at golf tournaments.

The connections she made there led her to jobs including the World Cup in 1993 in LA, after which she landed a stint as production manager on the skiing tour for 8 years. She also started doing football, which is where she noticed "The makeup artists were flakey, and sometimes didn't show up." One time in a pinch she ran to the drugstore, got some stuff and did it herself. Later, when another one showed up high at a game at the Orange Bowl, the producer turned to her again. This time she was ready, with a tackle box from Target filled with the necessary supplies. The producer let her double dip as a tech and a makeup artist (freelance slang for billing twice), but even better, she realized that was what she wanted to do.

She moved to LA to learn special effects makeup, and landed a job on "Unsolved Mysteries" with Robert Stack. Meantime she was picking up the art of blood and gore ("I can slash with the best of them!"), eventually working with director Steve Miner on the "Friday the 13th" movies. That led to stints on films such as "Forrest Gump," and an ever broadening set of contacts. She got a gig doing news in Austin, Texas, but found it boring. So when Sony records offered her a spot in New York as the house makeup artist for "Sessions at West 54th," she jumped at the chance. In that roll she worked with musicians from Elvis Costello to Sheryl Crow to Lou Reed and more. And those contacts led to much more on the New York scene and beyond.

But contacts only get you so far. It's about skills to be sure, not to mention attitude. "I treat everyone the same way," she told me. "I study their face for 20 seconds and I know what to do. I'm fast, I don't do things heavy and I don't play around. If they want to talk, I'll talk. I approach it as you are only as good as your last show; screw up once, that's what they will remember. And above all, I'm grateful for the work."

I asked her what her favorite gig was. Without hesitation, she said "The Tonys! Live show, live actors, no attitudes. They have no entourage, they are kind and appreciative of what I do." Her favorite person? "James Taylor. A real gentleman. He just says 'Hello Belinda' and I melt!" And with all the people she's met and jobs she's been on, I asked if there was anything she would like to do. For the first time, it took her a minute to respond. "I'd like to fly a plane." She laughed. "But professionally? I'm about to work with Lady Gaga and Tony Bennett. After that, what's left?" For Belinda, what's left indeed.

A Good Row

(2018)

Mick Dawson is headed to Hawaii; lucky guy, you might think. He is going there with his buddy Steve Sparkes, known as Sparky, and they plan on leaving on June 2nd from California. Jealous? After all, with the rough winter many of us have experienced it sounds like a trip any of us might enjoy. Well, consider a few notes to the journey. Depending on a number of factors the trip should take between 50 and 70 days. Their preferred mode of transport is a boat. And not just any boat, but a row boat. Mick and Steve will be one of six teams that will be crossing 2400 miles of ocean as part of the Great Pacific Race. Oh, and one other thing: Steve is blind.

So maybe you'll pass on this one.

Mick left his home in Brighton UK and is currently in San Francisco preparing mentally, physically and logistically for the race. While he's not approaching it lightly, it's not completely virgin territory for him either. He is an experienced adventurer, having crossed the Atlantic twice and circumnavigated the Falkland Islands in a kayak. A former Royal Marine, he is also in the Guinness Book of records as the skipper of the first and only rowing boat to cross the North Pacific from Japan to San Francisco. He did that in 2009 with his friend Chris Martin, a journey of 7000 miles that took more than six months.

Still, this particular crossing has special significance for him. "Sparky was invalided out of the Marines after losing his sight in the selection process for the Special Forces. In the 80's support for recovering veterans was limited to say the least, and it took ten years before he was given any rehabilitation. I'm glad to say that things have changed now with organizations like the two we're raising money for, The Royal Marines Charity and Blind Veterans UK."

On a personal level, Mick knows that feeling that comes with doing something truly special, and wants to share that: "I also think this will give Sparky something that was robbed of him when he was injured along with his sight. He will be the first blind person to row the Pacific. Already a legend in the 'Blind Veterans' community helping others, no one could be more worthy of being that first person than Sparky. It will be an honor to help him achieve that."

Of course, those are all laudable goals, but it still comes down to two guys in a rowboat in the middle of the ocean for more than a month. Not many people's idea of a good time. So why do it? For Mick, it dates back to the formative experience of turning 18 while serving in the Falklands War. "I had my birthday two days before the surrender, and had a highly sharpened appreciation for life, and how quickly it can end. For me it drove me to do something that mattered, and ocean rowing was it. It was a way to show that ordinary people can do extraordinary things." Or as he put it in the book he wrote about his epic North Pacific crossing, "The colours are never brighter than when you think you might be looking at them for the last time. That intensity of life can become addictive, and rowing oceans was how I dealt with that addiction."

Even though he knows the general gist of what he's getting into, Mick knows that there will be challenges: waves, sun, sharks and storms, not mention hours and hours of tedium as he and Sparky row and row and row. The race rules mandate that they do it all unaided, on their own for as long as it takes. They will be able to communicate and post their progress, and for the first time in the race's history, all crews are being provided with video cameras and the ability to upload footage along the way. Still, they will be alone, very alone. I asked Mick what he would miss the most. "There's part of me that wants to say nothing, which to a large degree is true. But obviously loved ones are the one thing you really miss and unsurprisingly appreciate more than ever." But he is an ex Royal Marine, so there is more: "showers, tea kettles, a comfy bed and a decent pint of Guinness!"

FOOD

The Price of a Slice

(2015)

The Big Apple is known for many things. The Empire State Building. Yankee Stadium. Broadway. Coney Island. The list goes on and on, almost too numerous to enumerate. And that's just the physical stuff. At least as many people come to New York to eat as to look. You name it, it's served here: French, Italian and Chinese, of course, but also Ethiopian and Caribbean, Barbeque and Cajun, Druze and Jerk. It's a plate of dreams: if you cook it, they will come.

Still, almost none of it beats a simple slice of pizza on the go. And that slice tastes even better when it only sets you back a buck. Mind you, I'm not saying that dollar pizza is empirically better than more expensive slices. I am saying that when you perform a high level quantitative analysis, and calculate price vs. value vs. epicurean satisfaction, it's hard to come out on the losing side of this particular equation.

I won't say I am hooked on the stuff, but am most certainly a user. So when I was running between appointments near Bryant Park in Manhattan, and had a few spare minutes at lunch time, I headed to Sixth Avenue where I knew there were a string of these establishments. But as I turned the corner, I stopped in my tracks.

The storefront I was aiming for was still there in all its rundown glory, but the sign up front now proudly proclaimed "Fresh Slice: $1.50." The planet had tilted on its axis.

To be fair, I never understood how they were able to sell a slice for a dollar. At eight slices to a pie, that's, let's see, eight dollars. A whole pie near me usually costs twice that, maybe more. Even allowing for the most bargain basement brands of sauce, cheese and flour, it's hard to see how you get the price down that low unless it's a Chinese knockoff procured via Ebay, which would take 4 weeks to get to you in a shoddy envelope. So a 50% markup was certainly more in keeping with the economic realities that must exist in the pizza making world. Still, it was as if someone had told me that Santa Claus wasn't for real.

Not wanting to accept this glacial shift without confirmation, I walked a few blocks further south to check out some of the shop's sisters. Sure enough, each had a sign out front confirming the new price point. Accepting the situation on the ground, I peeled three bills instead of two off my money clip, stuffed the two slices into my face, then popped a Tic Tac and headed to my meeting.

But as I started to think about it, I realized that all of these places had changed their price at the same time. While it's possible they were all owned by the same Pizza Cartel though some shadowy Cayman Islands blind trust, I suspected otherwise. True, they all seemed more or less clones of one another, and many even sported similar names: Fresh Pizza, Express Pizza, Fresh Express Pizza and so on. But several years ago I recalled a slice price war, where one establishment dropped their price and another matched it, then bested it. Detente was eventually reached, and the "about a dollar" price point was settled upon, with some places posting 99 cent signs, others slightly higher, though a crisp bill usually got you a slice regardless of what the sign stated.

So if they were indeed different establishments, were we talking price fixing on at least an urban scale? We've seen it in banks and milk, in airlines and art, so why wouldn't pizza slices be fair game for greed and market domination? To be fair, it you're going to try and control a market, the amount of risk and effort it takes seems antithetical to using pizza slices as your vehicle. But I guess that just shows how little vision I have as a robber baron.

These thoughts tumbled though my head over the next few days as I went about my usual business. Then once again I found myself racing between a meeting in midtown at noon and the garage where my car was parked. There, as I turned the corner on Eighth Avenue, was a stand and a sign that proudly proclaimed "$.99 Pizza." Maybe I was too hasty. Maybe there really is a Santa Claus.

Onion Ash and Burnt Corn

(2017)

Sometimes, all you want are some noodles.

Like many, we enjoy eating out. And while we have our favorites, in general we're pretty open. Chinese or Japanese, Indian or Italian, Greek or even Peruvian, if it has a menu (or even if it doesn't) we're gonna be just fine. Add in the old standbys of burgers, pizza, salads and sandwiches, and the one thing we won't do is starve.

That said, the hottest trend in restaurants is to push the envelope, along with the commensurate price. On the surface I'm fine with that; I enjoy trying new things in new ways, and don't mind paying for something that's demonstrably better. But we're talking about culinary sleights of hand that go well beyond a little extra spice here, or a new way of using cheese. Chefs are taking the building blocks of food, reducing them to their essence and even creating something from nothing. Or in the case we came across, nothing from something.

The restaurant that managed this feat was one of a bunch that served the "New Nordic" style of cooking. I guess that was to be expected, as we were in Copenhagen on holiday, and eating was one of our major activities. The city is full of these high-end inventive and expensive places, partly as an outgrowth of the Noma diaspora. That restaurant was ranked as the "best restaurant in the world" by Restaurant Magazine four times. And while it closed earlier this year, the chefs and staffers who worked there over the years have fanned out and tied to rekindle that same magic under new names.

On top of that, the aforementioned New Nordic manifesto turns out not to be an appellation bestowed by a critic, but an actual thing. In 2004, Claus Meyer, one of the founders of Noma and a sort of Danish James Beard crossed with Bobbie Flay, gathered together some top Scandinavian chefs. They penned a guide to raise the visibility and level of cuisine from their home countries, emphasizing local ingredients and traditional flavors in new ways, with an emphasis on "purity, simplicity & freshness." And so Noma began and begat Amass and Sletten and Barr and a hundred others, and has even landed on these shores with Meyer's own Agern and the Great Northern Food Hall at Grand Central.

But back to the food. Of those three guiding principles, I can most readily corroborate the last. Everything we tried was fresh, like it had just been made, baked, caught, dug up or plucked. As to purity, there were certainly no processed ingredients that stood out: the beef was beef, the chicken chicken and the grilled duck hearts were - well - we didn't try those, so can't say. But I would bet they were the real thing.

It's that last focal point with which I would take issue. To me, simplicity means just that: taking the component part as it is and, well, that's it. Yet these folks seemed to go out of their way to turn that on its head. For instance, the turkey with risotto and mushrooms was fine. It was the garnish of burnt corn that threw us. And not kennels, but popped, like you would find at the bottom of the Jiffy pan. Or the tuna with apple and – wait for it - elderflower & grilled kale. Yes, edible flowers and crispy leaves. And the aforementioned headturner for us, the grilled pork cheeks (don't ask) were topped with onion ash. Not onion itself, but the same roasted for hours until it turned black, then pulverized, turning to ash. Then again, I guess when you can order a dish described as "Bonito, Salted Turnip, Black Garlic, Dried Lambs Heart" you can't really act surprised when that's what they give you.

While all were interesting, and some better than others, dinner was somewhat exhausting. We tried to keep track and discern the various flavors and techniques, but it got to be overwhelming. And so one night we opted out and found a small Thai place. While the menu was in Danish, the owner was only too happy to help us translate it into English. And there we found red and green curries and noodles like we were used to. Unless you're from Bangkok, what does it say about your choices when Pad Thai turns out to be comfort food?

In Smoke We Trust

(2013)

We were setting up for a project with a gang that had been together many times. The clients were doing their thing, the techs theirs, each working in their own space and nodding politely to one other. My job, as usual, was bridging the divide between the two. As part of my rambling small talk, I asked one of the techs named Chris how his side business was going. He mentioned that the coming weekend would have him and his partners working their biggest event to date. One of the clients politely inquired over her shoulder as to the type of business they had. When Chris told her, conversation stopped. All turned to him, and they started swapping stories and tricks; it was all I could do to get us back on track. And the reason I lost control? Chis and his mates have a team that competes in professional BBQ.

BBQ is one culinary arena that inspires passion like no other; Mitch and Chris can wax philosophically about it for hours. Mitch says it best: "My whole life I was under the impression that BBQ was burgers, chicken, or even ribs drenched in sauce, then abused over super high heat on a propane grill. Never knew it was the exact opposite: taking your time, an all-day event, babysitting a hunk of meat in a smoke filled vessel, basting it until it becomes very tender, as it slowly caramelizes. Really putting some love into it. Very few things in life are worth that amount of time." Mind you, that's not his wife he's talking about, but a pork butt.

While Mitch got hooked at a shack in Atlanta called Daddy D's, Chris' epiphany was in 2009. "I met a guy named Tom Bera of Philly Blind Pig BBQ. Got a glimpse of his operation and I was hooked. Within the next year I bought a basic smoker from Home Depot and started learning. In 2011 we started competing in sanctioned events, and in 2012 I bought a tow behind Meadow Creek Barbecue TS250 smoker with a BBQ 42 Chicken cooker mounted on the front." Your daddy's Weber this is not.

Both guys have put some serious money and time into it, spending much of their off hours perfecting their technique, going to competitions, and more recently, selling their edible art at festivals. Their team, Zombie BBQ, won a bunch of awards over the past year or so, including 3rd in ribs at Smoke in the Valley in Green Lane, PA, 4th in brisket and 5th in pork at the New Holland Summerfest in New Holland, PA, and 4th in pork at Pork in the Park in Salisbury, MD.

Though the prize money does help offset an expensive hobby, competing isn't really about winning. Says Chris, "Everyone is really nice and willing to give you tips, tricks. It's a very friendly and fun environment. Every competition is like a mini vacation for us." However, it's a tiring vacation: "We start smoking around 8 pm on a Friday and run the pit all night until around 12 pm on Saturday. Since I usually have to feed the fire of my smoker ever hour or so, I don't get much sleep."

Each has their favorites. For Mitch, "Good brisket burnt ends can make your knees buckle, and great ribs are just a beautiful thing." Chris is a big brisket fan too, but has a few other specialties: "Something that I've been making lately for friends and family is pulled pork and Sriracha infused coleslaw egg rolls with hot pepper buffalo cheese, served with an oriental style BBQ sauce." No, you can't have his address.

In the documentary "American Smoke" that Mitch is making about the world of grillers, he opens the trailer with a shot of a bearded fellow competitor. Off camera Mitch asks, "Is barbequing better than sex?" The man gives a short laugh and the music starts. Some might think that laugh is there because the answer is that nothing could be better than carnal pleasures. But those in the know know better. The guy laughed for the simple reason that to many it's a rhetorical question. For them, the question isn't which position do you prefer, but do you like your ribs wet or dry. For them, BBQ and sex are merely two flavors of the same thing; it's just a matter of what produces the smoke.

Hot, Hotter

(2014)

You know the scene. Tom Cruise, as a young, gung-ho military lawyer, confronts a snarling Jack Nicholson, playing a ramrod straight officer running Guantanamo Bay in "A Few Good Men." Cruise, as Lt. (j.g.) Daniel Kaffee, prods Nicholson as Colonel Nathan Jessup on the stand. Jessup snaps back at Kaffee, "You want answers?!" to which Kaffee responds, "I want the truth!" In one of the most iconic lines ever, Jessup thunders back, "You can't handle the truth!"

My situation was almost the same. Except it was not a trial and I am not a lawyer, merely a person getting some lunch. The guy behind the counter was no officer, just someone taking orders. And we weren't talking about truth, we were talking about chicken.

Hot chicken to be precise. Philadelphia may have its cheesesteak and New Orleans its po'boy, but if you are in Nashville, you must find time to try the city's culinary specialty. There are a couple of places nationwide that have tried to gain a toehold selling the stuff, but they are few and far between. To get this particular variant you really have to go to the mother churches found in Music City USA.

The basics are simple: you take some chicken, marinade it in buttermilk, coat it with flour, then pan or deep fry it. After cooking, a paste made of lard and spices is rubbed onto the pieces. Consisting of some combination of sugar, garlic and cayenne pepper, the trick is to impart both flavor and heat. The result is served on thick slices of white bread accompanied by slices of dill pickle.

Of course, it's called hot chicken not because of the temperature. Most places make it at varying heats per the wishes of the consumer. At the bottom of the scale is something mildly akin to regular fried chicken. At the other end is something that one reviewer describes as "crying-from-your-eyes-and-nostrils-and-other-orifices kind of heat. Your tongue will curl up in the corner, and pray for death's swift, sweet kiss." Yeah, it's that hot.

Being one who likes spicy food, I thought I could handle something in the middle. So I decided to have my "come to chicken" moment at a place called 400 Degrees, where you order your heat in hundred degree increments. When it was my turn, I requested an order of chicken strips, a side of coleslaw and an iced tea. The gentlemen dutifully wrote it down, then asked me my heat preference. I replied, "Well, I like hot Buffalo wings, so how about 200?" He looked me up and down, sized me up as a newbie, and channeling Colonel Jessup said, "Son, these are no Buffalo wings."

I'm sure he saw the deflation and hurt on my face, because he quickly changed his tone. "Tell you what. Strips come in three, so I will give you two 100 degree pieces, and one 200 degree. And if that 200 isn't too much, you come back and we'll step you up. How's that?" I readily agreed to this face saving compromise. I paid my tab, and went to sit down and wait.

A while later they brought me a tray. Two of the pieces had a rosy glow, but one was ruby in color. To start, I cut off a piece of the lighter colored strip. It was powerful stuff, flavorful and vibrant, a taste that made you sit up and take notice. After I did a little palate cleansing with the coleslaw, I took aim at the 200. It barely got it into my mouth before my eyes teared up and my nose started running. It had flavor, to be sure. But mixed with that flavor was fire. My tongue tingled, my ears started ringing and all I could think was, My God, what must 400 be like?

Still, I alternated back and forth, enjoying both variations, grateful for the ice cubes in my cup. The guy from the counter walked by and smiled. He returned a few moments later with a small tray. "You look a nice guy, so we made you another piece," he said. Between sips of tea, I thanked him profusely as he put it in front of me, praying to the Lord above that the new piece was colored to the century mark and no higher. Buffalo, forgive me, but you have been bested.

Art to Eat

(2017)

My dad was a buyer for department stores, and among other things, was responsible for candy. Once he took my sister and me with him to the Philadelphia Candy Show, where the latest products and equipment were showcased. For me, the most magical thing was an enrobing machine. A slowly moving conveyor belt carried whatever you put on it through a chocolate waterfall. I stood there making chocolate-covered soda crackers for as long as Dad let me. If there was a heaven on earth, this was it. We were literally kids in a candy store.

That came back to me as I stood in Joan Coukos' workshop and facility. The owner of Chocolat Moderne, her 9th floor production space in New York is a place where dreams are made. A self-professed foodie, she grew up in a Greek household eating unusual foods: "Calf brains and caviar at six!" But she was more eater than cook: her mother and grandmother wouldn't let her into the kitchen because she made such a mess.

Dual degrees in in Russian and French from Duke, and an MBA from UNC led her into international finance and a lot of travel, and she eventually became a banker in Moscow for three years.

Enroute to Belgium for a vacation, she read an article about chocolatier Pierre Marcolini, a top pastry chef in Europe who treated his chocolate creations like fine pastries. Once in Brussels, while taking a stroll through the market at La Place du Grand Sablon, she stumbled upon some antique chocolate molds, and was stricken. She saw it as a sign, pointing her in a new direction.

She returned to New York, and starting learning all she could about making chocolates. In her tiny apartment she made batch after batch, her co-workers being the beneficiary of her experiments. "I knew this was it. I had a million ideas, I trusted my palate and I had a lot of confidence." She did research, took classes and sought advice from food luminaries like Danny Meyer of Union Square Café. Each step brought her a little closer to her goal. Eventually a reorganization at the bank led to layoffs. Deciding it was now or never, she took her severance and savings, and in 2003 started Chocolat Moderne.

Her goal was to combine her loves of food and art, making chocolates that were delicious, unusual and beautiful. Working in small handmade batches, she uses premium Valrhona chocolate as the base, adding flavors and fillings she creates. For the eyes, she and her staff hand-paint the chocolates with colored cocoa butter, some with Jackson Pollack drippings, others with Peter Max swirls.

Then there're the tastes. Her original assortment, now in its twelfth year, includes her signature flavors of grapefruit, single-malt scotch and raspberry. But she has gone far beyond those with her Kimono Collection, featuring chocolates with Shiso Lime, Matcha Green Tea and Soy Miso flavors, and her Greek Revival assortment, showcasing caramels with Kalamata Olive flavoring, others infused with Pomegranate and Rose Water.

Her originality and quality have won her numerous awards, features on TV and distribution in high end stores like Barneys, Saks, and Dean and Deluca, whose Japanese catalog this month features Chocolat Moderne on the cover. She's also moving into new channels, including being featured in Amazon Prime's Surprise Sweets program, a special chocolate offering at Starbucks and premium chocolate distributer Chococurb.

I asked Joan what she wants people to get from her chocolates. "I want it to be memorable," she says. "It should start when you see it: first you eat with your eyes. And the taste has to be unique, like no other." She wants to keep growing, but only as long as she can maintain the quality. And she has ideas. The next big thing? She smiles: "I don't like to say ahead of time. But I have my eye on an ingredient that's always been popular, but in a new way."

Joan proudly points to a high shelf in the front of her space. There, nestled next to a display of trophies she's won, are the two antique molds that started it all. And I realized that the feeling I got as a kid sending crackers through that chocolate waterfall is the same she gets when she makes her creations. The difference? I was a kid in a candy store. Joan's still a kid at heart, and she owns the store.

Green Rush, Ground Floor

(2015)

It's not like Laurie Wolf really planned on being in on the ground floor. A chef who trained at the Culinary Institute of America, she authored a number of successful cookbooks and worked as a food editor and stylist when she lived on the East Coast. Seeking to get out of the New York craziness, she and her family moved to Portland, Oregon, where she continued doing much the same, including authoring a well-received book named "The Portland, Oregon Chef's Table."

Laurie also has a seizure disorder which she found was treatable with marijuana. And with Oregon being one of the first states to pass a medical marijuana law in 1998, she was able to do something legally there that she was unable to do in the Empire State. Then one time at a dispensary Laurie decided to try some alternative forms of the drug, packaged as edible brownies. Her expert opinion? "They tasted horrible." And so she started experimenting, seeing if she could successfully marry the different highs you get from chocolate and pot.

Then this past July Oregon joined Colorado, Washington state, Alaska and the District of Columbia in legalizing recreational use of the drug. The so-called "Green Rush" was on, and suddenly lots of people were trying to see how they could have a finger in what is expected to be a multi-billion dollar brownie. And standing in the middle of it all was Laurie, having already baked it.

She started a company called "Laurie and MaryJane," and developed recipes for a variety of foods. All are organic, additive- and preservative-free, and have a consistent dosage of THC, the most psychoactive ingredient in Cannabis. There is a Fudgy Brownie of course, but also Almond Cake Bites and a Sweet n' Savory Nut mix, Peanut Butter, Cannabutter (a fusion of cannabis and butter), and Cannacoconut oil for cooking and baking. They have fun and funny sayings on the packaging like, "Go fudge yourself" and "Some of my best friends are nuts!." And not to brag or anything, but they are so good that the nuts placed first and the almond bites second in their respective categories at this year's Fourth Annual Dope Cup in Seattle.

Some might see Laurie's world as the ultimate kid in the candy store. She allows it's pretty great, but there are some downsides. "The testing and tasting has been challenging since I have gotten high when I need to be working. Aside from medicating for my seizure disorder which does not get me high, I only indulge in the evenings. Too many bad cases of the munchies!" Still, it's a business, and she has to make it work: "I can take a small taste or two and not get high. But just that. A whole one of our bites will be too strong. I know how much I can eat at this point." I asked her if she ever got tired of it: "I don't get sick of weed, so many different strains to try with different flavor profiles. In fact, I often make our products unmedicated for giveaways and demos, and never tire of the taste."

Aside from the product itself, one really unexpected upside of the new business is how she has involved her family. Her son's fiancé Mary does marketing, designs all the packaging and helps with production, while her husband Bruce, a well-known photographer, shoots the mouthwatering product shots. She smiled: "Having it all in the family is pretty terrific. I call us the Wolf Cartel."

I asked Laurie what she hoped people get from her products. Her answer echoes her own experiences: "I hope they get enjoyment from the high and the taste, but also relief from pain, anxiety, discomfort and life, if that's what they need." Beyond that, she's very proud of what is happening in Oregon and her part in it: "Portland is an amazing city and I love that it is so progressive. I hope that we do marijuana right. I was on the subcommittee for edibles for the Oregon Liquor Control Commission. My hope is that the OLCC will support small cannabis businesses and let the roll out set an example for the rest of the country."

There are precious few opportunities any person ever gets to see something truly cutting edge, be it a piece of technology or a new social movement. This is one of those moments, and Laurie doesn't just have a ring side seat, she is a player. She shakes her heads and laughs about it: "It is great. I am learning so much. And to see this happen in my life is fantastic."

Can I Have Another?

(2016)

It was a joke. Not a "funny, ha ha" kind of joke, but a "bears no relation to reality" kind of joke. It wasn't meant to be, of course. It was just trying to do the right thing, offering sensible guidance to any person who picked up the container and read the back panel. And while it could have been a jar of peanut butter or a bag of pretzels, it was a box of fish. Red fish. Swedish fish, to be exact.

If you're connoisseur of high end confectioneries, if you can tell the difference between a chocolate truffle from Godiva and one from Lindt, if you buy your candy by the piece vs. the pound, then you might wonder what I'm talking about. Tuna or sardines might come in a can, but what kind of fish comes in a box? But if you are like me, and are well versed in gratuitous sugary nibbles, then you know all too well this grandchild of Tootsie Rolls, cousin of Root Beer Barrels and Smarties, and close sibling of Red Hot Dollars and Gummi Worms. As a person who waxed rhapsodically in this space not once but twice about Peeps, I feel uniquely qualified to weigh in on this topic. And if you don't know what Peeps are, then we most definitely travel in different circles.

But let's get back to the joke of the fish.

Knowing my weak spot for anything that has a preponderance of sugar as its main ingredient, a friend's wife was nice enough to buy a small box of Swedish fish to have around as a snack for when we were working. So called because Malaco, the company that created them was indeed Swedish, and well, the fishing industry in that country was very large, the candy was developed specifically for the US and Canadian markets back in the 1950's. The slightly squishy soft pieces, each in the shape of a miniature cod-esque aquarian, are known in their native tongue as "pastellfiskar," or pale-colored fishes. And no, in spite of their heritage, while the taste is vaguely cherry-like, neither is it reminiscent of lingonberry.

They are just sugary, chewy tidbits that taste like, well, red and stick to your teeth. Eat one, and you'll eat another. And another. And yet one more. And that's where the joke comes in. On the box it says there are "about" 2 servings per container, each about 7 pieces. But that's a cruel metric: those fishies are like crack. Have one and your body hungers for another. Even as you pry it from your fillings, the box beckons you to take more. Saying a mere catch is only 7 is a pipe dream. Sure. Like that's gonna happen.

But there is nod to reality if you read further. For while the "suggested" serving size is 7 pieces, there is another column. And that one bows to reality, or at least, my version of it. So while the nutritional tallies are roughly double the single serving, it doesn't say "Two Servings." It says "Entire Box." Which is generally what I eat.

I'm not proud of it, but it's the way it is. It's like when the box of cookies says "Serving Size 2 Cookies" as opposed to "Entire Tray." Or when the jar of peanuts says "Serving Size 1 Ounce" as opposed to "Two or Three Handfuls." Thankfully, pizza boxes just say "You've tried the rest, now try the best." Because if they said "Serving Size One Slice" I'd be embarrassed as I would be caught consuming "Most of the Pie."

You can post all the calories counts you want. You can show me the food pyramid in four colors, with delicious looking pictures of whole grains and leafy greens. My wife can have lots of fresh fruit in the fridge, chilled just the way I like it. And I'll gladly try and do the right thing, cutting down on saturated fats and increasing my intake of veggies. But if you honestly think that telling me that 7 Swedish fish is all I'm supposed to eat, the only way that's going to happen is if you tie my hands. Just please do it with licorice whips. I love those.

It Ain't a Party

(2013)

If you go to a party, you expect certain things. You expect there to be drinks, both alcoholic and non-alcoholic. You expect music, usually of the recorded variety, but occasionally a live performer. You expect other people, some you might know, others you're meeting for the first time. And best of all (at least for me) you expect something to eat.

Maybe it's because you don't have to do anything other than pick it up and put it in your mouth, party food always tastes good. Unless it's your party and you get bogged down in the preparation (and even then you can ask others to bring stuff), it's as much a reason to go as the people or the occasion. Strike that; it is THE reason to attend. Doesn't matter if it's a bowl of nuts or a piece of sushi, a mini cupcake or a piece of chicken on a toothpick. All that is required is the ability to juggle a napkin, a small plate and a half filled glass, while simultaneously stuffing something in your mouth. It's a true walk-and-chew mini-quiche at the same time moment.

As to the food itself, it almost doesn't matter. At one I went to recently there was everything from apple turnovers to pizza to some kind of individual-serving-in-a-plastic-cup of a broccoli salad in a vinaigrette, surprisingly tasty in spite of its presentation. Another more high-end gathering included a full raw bar, artisanal breads and dips, and sliced-to-order fillet of beef. Still another included these little chicken things, as well as some kind of round, breaded, fried... well, actually, I'm not sure what was inside, but it was mighty tasty. The bottom line is that I didn't starve at any of them.

For while I may have to force myself out of my comfort zone so as not stand in one place and instead, circulate to chat and meet people, I have no similar reticence with the victuals. I start at one end of the room, and plot a circuitous course to the other. Along the way I take a bite or two of everything and anything. And if the food is being passed, I use what little trigonometry I remember to calculate the intersection point between myself and the moving wait staff, the better to snag the stuff hot out of oven. Hockey great Wayne Gretsky famously said he didn't skate to where the puck was, but to where it would be. I do the same, just with mini-eggrolls.

That being said, while you might fault me for not being discriminating in my consumption, I do have favorites. I love cheeses, and would happily spend the entire party trying one after the other from those big mirrored platters accented with grapes and dried apricots. A good iced seafood spread is hard to tear yourself away from, whether it includes sushi, shrimp, clams or oysters. And if there's an assortment of desserts, rest assured that I will try every one, even if it means I take just one bite of Key Lime pie, then put it discretely on a waiter's passing tray, only to repeat the same with a serving of the apple spice cake.

But there is one thing that turns my knees to utter jelly when it makes an appearance. Yes, I enjoy spinach balls, have learned to like pâté and can appreciate a sprinkling of caviar as a garnish. But if I see them put out a plate of pigs-in-blankets, well, you better clear a path.

I know that individually it's not much. Just a little hot dog, an object of dubious pedigree at best. A piece of dough, puff pastry if you're lucky, but the biscuit variety in a pinch. And spicy mustard, sometimes designer with seeds in it, though Gulden's brown is actually best. But together? Together it's heaven. It's peanut butter and jelly, it's french fries and ketchup, it's popcorn and butter. It's something that just, well, works.

Let me be clear: if you're inviting me over for any reason I'm happy to come. I'll happily eat your savory cheese truffles with chives. And I'll be sure to try those crispy zucchini blossoms. And no doubt those prosciutto, mozzarella and basil roll-ups you got from that little deli sound delicious. But you ain't got pigs in blankets? Well, I'm not so sure you can really call it a party.

TRAVEL

Big, Bigger, Biggest

(2015)

With my unexpected day off in Fort Worth, I could have just stayed in my hotel room. I could have walked around downtown and poked my nose into a museum or two. I could have seen a movie, or taken a bike ride, or caught up on some work. But it was that 24-day period when there are cattle to be judged, barbeque sauce to be sampled and Snickers bars to be deep fried. And so I went to the Texas State Fair.

Like everything in the state, the Fair is defined by its scale. If you go to your local carnival, you expect to see a few rides, some hot dog stands, and a couple of games of chance. Supersize the above, throw in some livestock judging and handicrafts competitions, and you've got most State Fairs around the country. But inject all that with steroids, add a massive 400 vehicle auto show featuring pickup after pickup, two grudge-match college football games (Grambling vs Prairie View A&M and Texas vs Oklahoma), corn dogs, turkey legs and deep-fried everything, and you've got the Lone Star version.

Held every year since 1886 with a few time outs during World Wars, the fair surrounds the Cotton Bowl stadium on nearly

300 acres. But the above listing is just a start: there are museums, 7 concert venues, pig races, an Aquarium, a Sky Tram, and a 55-foot-tall Big Tex talking statue, to name but a few of the other attractions. While officials don't bother to tally day to day figures, they generally host over 3 million people annually, making it the biggest such exposition in the nation.

Everything is on a colossal scale. The midway takes a full 30 or 40 minutes to walk down, with games of every stripe beckoning to be played. You can win prizes ranging from the typical small stuffed animals to plush toys bigger that you, from electric guitars to furniture. There are easily a dozen fun houses and 70 rides, with at least half of those designed to induce nausea. Some are versions of ones you've likely seen, like Scrambler and Roundup, but rocket fuel injected in both scale and action. And some are simply death defying: one called SlingShot looks like a massive construction crane that simply straps two people to the end, and then flips end over end. That privilege cost 70 tickets, or $35 dollars, but you do get a POV video of your terrified reaction as a souvenir.

Of course, with livestock being such a central part of Texas' legacy, there were heifers and goats and swine a plenty. I was there on Future Farmers of America day, and watched judging by the next generation of cattle barons. Where else could you hear 20-year old Blayze Bierschwale from Lampasas, TX explain about the Santa

Gertudis cattle being shown: "Number 4 is a more feminine heifer that's smoother about her shoulders, a bit softer about her hardened flank." But she paled compared to his favorite: "Number 1 is little bit straighter about her hock, a really feminine good balanced female. And when you get behind her you can see she's light constructed and stout." Now, THAT'S pillow talk.

But if the Fair is known for anything, it's the food. The staples are corn dogs, piles of french fries that size of Stetsons topped with cheese, chili and barbeque sauce, and massive grilled turkey legs that look like they belong on the Flintstones. If it can be dunked in batter and fried, you can find it there: Oreos, stuffed olives, cheesecake, pumpkin pie, PB&J, spaghetti and even lemonade (No, I have no idea how they actually do that). And each year there are specials that go where no food has gone before. This year that included a Smoky Bacon Margarita, Deep Fried Cappuccino and the Krispy Kreme Donut Burger.

When they remade the movie "State Fair" for the third time in 1962, they moved the setting from Iowa to Dallas. And while there's still a Tilt-A-Whirl and maybe even a pig named Blue Boy, times have changed. If they went today, Pat Boone, Booby Darren and Ann Margaret might have some chicken-fried lobster, or a maybe a pork chop on a stick, but only if they left room for some deep fried chocolate bacon. Big Tex would expect no less.

Thinking in Generations

(2015)

Having just returned from a trip to the Netherlands, I can confidently say that there is much to like. The people are warm and friendly, the cafes plentiful and welcoming. Lots of museums dot Amsterdam and other cities, and the dress code is casual in just about every venue. It's a relatively safe country, although it must be said that you do take your life in your hands anytime you step off the curb and do battle with the bikes, scooters, trams, buses and cars that zip around with abandon. To be fair, there are some questionable practices: with such treats as herring and cheese, one wonders about the population's fascination with licorice, so much so that they are the world leader in consumption at about four pounds a year per head. Still, even if hash brownies and legal prostitution are your measure of forward progress, while you certainly have a different scale than mine, the country is still a most welcoming place.

But perhaps one of its most attractive qualities isn't any of these things. While I'm sure that the locals have plenty of their own "inside the beltway" spats and issues, it's refreshing to see how united a country can be on a single issue. True, that issue is literally their very survival in a most literal sense. But to see what they have done and what they continue to do to hold the sea at bay is not only an engineering achievement of the first order, but a demonstration of what can happen when people look beyond next month and next year, and set their sights on a time frame of generations.

It's not like they have a choice. More than a quarter of the country lies below sea level. Throughout their history, this small country, which contains the estuaries of the rivers Rhine, Meuse and Scheldt, has fought an ongoing battle with the forces of nature. More than once people and land have been flooded out by a combination of storms and tides. Think of New York and Sandy, or New Orleans and Katrina. Now expand that image to an entire country, and you begin to get the picture.

While dikes have been used almost since people settled there, it was in the last century that the process accelerated. The nearly 20 mile long Afsluitdijk dike was finished in 1932, and created a vast inland sea in the center of the country called the Ijsselmeer. More efforts followed, with new urgency coming after a disastrous flood in 1953 in the southern part of the country that killed over 1800 people and flooded over 600 square miles. Since then, miles and miles of new structures have been put in place, in some cases to protect the land that is there, while in others the goal is to try and reclaim that which the sea formerly took possession.

It sounds like something from a science fiction movie about colonizing a new planet, but the Dutch are very proud of their New Land. By first damming the water, then pumping it out, they started the slow but steady program of creating virgin ground. A look at a map shows this accelerating addition of space used for both agriculture and housing. Drive as we did through the countryside, and the locals never tire of pointing out what used to be under water that is now a field, a park, a factory, or a housing development. They never tire of it, because it's a process they never stop. They can't: to do so is surrender to a force which has no mercy.

Above the entrance to the engineering building at the University of Wyoming is chiseled "Strive On – The Control of Nature is Won, Not Given." In that light, the Dutch have asked for nothing for which they aren't willing to fight. Yes, it costs immense amounts of money and manpower. Yes, there is much debate about which plan to follow. Yes, there are those that are unhappy with changes which threaten decades old patterns of living. But sometimes you have to take the long view. It's hard, but they've done it. In this country we excel at disaster relief in so many different areas. It would be nice if we at least occasionally put the cart before the horse, learned from the Dutch, and looked at ways of avoiding disaster in the first place.

7% Growth

(2015)

One of the first pieces I ever wrote for this space related to a trip I made to Hong Kong back in 1995. Indeed, it was actually a series of email letters I wrote to family and friends on that trip that formed the basis for that column. Titled "Where First meets Third," it focused on the unique spot the city occupied at the intersection of the developed world and the developing. I wrote about the bamboo scaffolding used to build skyscrapers, and the computer shops that were cheek and jowl with shops featuring live chickens. And I marveled at the frantic energy and vitality of a place that seemed to be inventing itself on the spot.

Twenty years later, as I write this on a plane coming back from my most recent excursion there, I'm struck by how many of the themes I noted 20 years ago are still the same, even if the balance seems to have shifted a bit.

Of course, the biggest change is the fact that the city is no longer owned by the British, having been handed back to the Chinese in 1997. That said, even though it reports to a communist master, it retains its separate and special status as a capitalist outpost. Indeed, it practices, flaunts and displays its economic freedom like few other places in the world. Buildings that were new waterfront property when I was there two decades ago are gone, or pushed inland by the expansion not only of the economy but of the very ground on which it is built. You see it happening before your eyes: as I got off the Star Ferry, I watched a fleet of bulldozers push load after load of dirt into the water with the goal of creating even more land.

As one person said to me, "this is what 7% growth looks like." Sure, there are tenement apartments with laundry fluttering from windows, not to mention the occasional foodstuff. But more and more you see new high rises, some gleaming, some more functional. Hardly a block goes by that doesn't have construction, with some sites taking up hectare after hectare. That adds to traffic which was already legendary: even pedestrians can face a detour of several blocks just to get to the other side of the street.

The wealth that flows into the city has led to the creation of a huge number of high-end marble, glass and steel shopping malls populated by luxury brand stores. Somebody must be buying, but most look empty, staffed by bored clerks whiling away the time among the Channel bags and Tiffany jewelry and Manolo shoes by tapping endlessly on their smartphones. The old rabbit warren of stores in Kowloon still exists, but among the tailor shops and noodle counters are Starbucks counters and Samsung galleries.

And while the Ladies and Temple street markets have become even more infested with knockoff handbags and "copy watches," you can still find the locals shopping at butchers in Wan Chai who display their wares as a bloody meat-wall along the street, or at stalls in Apliu street featuring cheap clothing, interspersed with other specialty sellers, one with old tools, one selling nothing but magnets, another displaying hundreds of old remote controls.

There're lots more of these collisions of old and new. The WiFi is ubiquitous, and the electronic gadgets plentiful and cheap. The MTR, the local subway, still astounds with its gleaming stations and trains with no partitions between cars, creating seemingly endless hallways gliding along. Restaurants flaunting Michelin stars seem everywhere, with prices seeming even more stratospheric because of the nearly 8 to 1 exchange rate.

But just a few streets away from all that you can find grubby booths with a few rickety tables doling out bowls of soup and piles of prawns for just a few dollars. There are still stalls with live chickens and frogs just waiting to be dinner. And next to a vendor displaying computer cables is an old man selling a collection of old shoes, some pictures, a wooden flute and a wheelchair.

There was talk of the world taking an Asian pivot, a Chinese 21st century. To be sure, it's pretty early in the game to tell if that characterization will stand the test of time. But Hong Kong isn't waiting. It's still First and Third, but the former is most definitely squeezing the out the latter.

St. Petersburg 101 (Part 1)

(2010)

In our circle of acquaintances, it's not uncommon to know those who travel outside these shores. The locations vary: Western Europe is a usual destination, as are South and Latin America, and the major cities of the Far East. But tell someone you're going to Russia, and even among experienced road warriors you'll likely get a raised eyebrow or two. But with our youngest spending a semester there, it offered us an excuse to try something very different. And so we journeyed to St. Petersburg to spend a week and get a sense of the place.

Anyone guidebook will tell you the basics. A very manageable city on the Gulf of Finland, it sports such major attractions as the Hermitage, one of the great art museums of the world. Also not to be missed, (and we didn't) are St. Isaac's Cathedral, The Peter and Paul Fortress and The Church of the Savior on Spilled Blood. Add in the Kirov ballet, a few blini and some vodka, and a journey outside the city to Peterhof, the summer palace of Peter the Great whose grounds and gravity-fed fountains are one of the wonders of the world, and you have a trip for the memory books.

But what follows are a few more personal impressions of the place beyond a blow by blow of the premier attractions. By no means definitive, it's some of the things that struck us as we walked... and walked and walked and walked... around the core of the city and to a few outlying areas. Colored by our own biases and experiences, while also being almost comically selective as to what made an impression on us, it is none the less what we remember most once we strip away the simple recitation of where we went and what we saw. For this week, the focus will be on the physical sense of place; next, on the people.

The first thing that caught our eye was the colors. Many of the buildings are mint green or soft pink or pale yellow or baby blue. Whether it is indeed to make them stand out from the snow as we were told, or for some other reason, it gives the city a certain fairytale quality which contrasts mightily with what you expect from a place that is so associated with historical repression.

But if the buildings are colorful, the crowds certainly are not. The people are almost exclusively white and European looking. You see slight variations from Slav to Nordic ("Piter" itself being 40 minutes by plane from Helsinki) to some slight Mongolian influence. But you literally see no dark or truly Asian faces walking down the street. Meanwhile, the clothes and shoes are 180 degree opposites of that. Yes, it is a city, but dark tones don't just predominate, they overwhelm. We passed many a store sporting huge collections of boots and shoes that Henry Ford would have appreciated: you could have any color as long as it was black.

The streets and sidewalks were pleasantly wide and the buildings refreshingly low, making it feel similar to and yet somehow different from other European cities. Part of that can be attributed to the fact that it was all but demolished in the great Siege of 1941-1945 and then rebuilt, a memory still fresh both individually and institutionally. Indeed, we were shown explosive damage from the war marked with a plaque, and further afield passed a bomb shelter adjacent to a haunting cemetery filled with war dead, whose headstones were each miniature coffins filled with fresh flowers.

But if the canals and rivers felt like Amsterdam, and the many parks and squares like London, the numerous onion dome churches and signs in Cyrillic reminded you that you are in a place the hails from a different heritage than the west. The alphabet conspires to make it all but impossible to discern at first glance what's on a given street. That being said, we were able to finally decipher the hieroglyphics enough to know the places where we could get a bite (кафе) and the ubiquitous food shops which were open around the clock (24 часа). And we noted that "yucas" only seem to come in sets of 24.

Space won't allow a full reporting of impressions made over the entire week, but there are plenty more: the leftover Soviet era buildings, the brand new sleek Mercedes contrasting with the barely running ancient Ladas, the brides posing with their husbands in front of almost every major landmark. Suffice it to say it was indeed far different than what we were used to. And the people? That, comrades, will have to wait till next week. Until then, das vadanya.

St. Petersburg 101 (Part 2)

(2010)

Last week in this space I related impressions we had on a recent visit to St. Petersburg, Russia. In that brief report, the focus was on the place and the sights we saw. In this outing I'll try and get less physical and more personal, in talking about the people in general and one set of encounters in particular.

Whenever you travel, you have to remember that, like Blanche DuBois, you depend on the kindness of strangers. And by and large all we met were friendly and helpful. True, the old babushkas working the registers in the little grocery stores or selling tokens in the Metro (for 22 rubles each, about 73 cents) had an attitude that anything other than exact change was an insult. But beyond that, mime and pointing and a few words of pidgin Russian managed to get us food, directions, admission and the occasional fresh "peeshka" or donut covered in sugar.

But without a doubt our most memorable encounters were two evenings spent with our son's host family. While he is studying in St. Petersburg for the fall semester, they provide him a room and 2 meals a day. They have accepted him warmly and eased his transition into the culture, for which we are very grateful. So when we were planning our trip, we suggested to him that we would love to thank them by buying them dinner at a local restaurant.

They accepted the invitation and made reservations at a homey Georgian place. Dinner was a fun and lively affair (and delicious as well), and we were taken when halfway through they invited us to join them several nights later in their flat for a home cooked meal. It's the kind of encounter that no organized tour can ever hope to duplicate.

Elena is a private teacher of English, while Andrei works in advertising. Her English is excellent, while he understands more than he speaks. Their daughter Nastia (short for Anastasia) and her boyfriend Igor are both students, she in psychology and he in computers and art, and both had a far better grasp of our tongue then we did of theirs.

Their flat was small, three rooms plus a kitchen and bathroom. Like many Russians they have a dacha about an hour out of the city, though it has no heat and is very rustic. It does have apple trees which provided fruit for the wonderful tart Elena made to accompany the borscht, vodka, wine and tea we shared around the table in their living room. To us they seemed typically middle class, and indeed by the end of the evening we lamented the fact we didn't live closer to one another.

Our conversations went in fits and starts, as we shifted topics and languages, with plenty of sidetracks to translate both literal words and cultural ideas. They talked with pride about the history of their country, and the hardships in particular the people of St. Petersburg endured during the war, a memory still surprisingly fresh. They lamented how the police are corrupt and not to be trusted, and marveled as to how our experience in the US is so radically different. We talked about how money and power drive governments and actions, though they have all but given up hope that they have any impact on theirs, while we take it as an article of faith that we have a say in ours.

They have a skewed view of the U.S., driven by the images they see in American films and videos, and have a hard time understanding our diversity and openness. That said, it is their dream to visit this country, particularly New York and the Grand Canyon. Unfortunately, visa issues make it exceedingly difficult for individual Russians to come just to tour.

But our time together was also filled with shared experiences as much as pointing out contrasting cultures. Andrei, who has a background as a musician, was encouraged by Elena to sing a haunting Russian folk song. He then played the piano in their apartment, as did their daughter and our older son. We looked at family photos and swapped recipes: she told me how to make the apple tart we enjoyed, and my wife gave them recipes for chili. And we struggled to explain what a marshmallow was, and why in its Fluff form it tastes great on the peanut butter we all love.

It's hard and probably foolish to extrapolate from this individual encounter to anything beyond what it was: a gathering of two families from different cultures and countries and the search for common ground. But we found just that. And as big as the world is, it reminded us that it can be a small place, and we do best when we treat it as such.

"Welcome to Our Country"

(2010)

I had just flown back into Newark airport, and was heading straight into Manhattan to go to work. The fastest way to do that is to catch the shuttle train that circles the airport, then connect to a regular train to the city. I have to assume that space limitations dictated design when they built the Airlink system: the cars are small and cramped, with each consisting of 2 small unconnected cabins. In practice this means it feels less like a subway and more like a horizontal elevator.

The good news was that the airport was relatively uncrowded. I moved to the front of the platform, and when the train arrived I hopped into the empty first cabin. There I settled onto the lone bench seat for the 10 minute ride to the station where I would make my connection.

At the next terminal, the doors opened and a red-coated customer service agent got on pulling a cart piled with luggage, followed by an older gentleman. She motioned for the man to sit next to me. "Where are you going?" she asked me without preamble. I responded that I was headed to the station. "OK," she said as she looked at him and pointed at me, "Get off where he does." She looked at me as the chime rang to indicate that the doors were closing. "There'll be another agent meeting him at the other end," she said as she jumped off quickly.

Great, I thought, now he's my responsibility. I looked at him more closely: he was elderly, very thin and Indian. I smiled; he smiled back. "Thank you," he said in said in a soft, accented voice. "It's no trouble," I replied. I asked him where he was coming from. "I just came from India. And this is my first visit here." Suddenly my attitude changed. He was no longer a burden: more to the point, I was now an ambassador. Without thinking, I said the first thing that popped into my mind: "Well, welcome to our country."

He smiled broadly. "Thank you," he said. "I am very excited to be here." We continued talking. He had flown for 16 hours, and was going to take the train to Philadelphia, where he would be staying with friends. I asked him where in India he was from: he answered with a name I couldn't pronounce nor remember. I asked him how hold he was: 83 was his response. "God bless you, sir," I said. "It takes a lot of courage at your age to travel this far alone." He nodded: "Yes, at least I am healthy and can do this."

As we progressed, I pointed out the Newark and New York skylines. I told him I hoped he would have a chance to visit other places as well as Philadelphia, as our country has many interesting sights. With great pride, he said, "Our country is very diverse as well. Have you ever been to India?" I confessed I had not, but told him I always wanted to. I also told him I loved Indian food, which brought another big smile.

By now we were pulling into the station. Of course, no agent was waiting for us. He looked concerned as I helped him maneuver his trolley and luggage off the train. I told him not to worry: I would get him to the right place. We made our way to the elevator. As we rode up, he looked at me and said, "I am so lucky to have met you." I said it was no problem, but he must do the same for me when I finally came to his country. He grinned, and said "I would be honored."

When we stepped off the elevator, an agent was walking past. I asked her if she could help him purchase the correct ticket and get him to the right platform. She nodded and turned to first help another couple. I moved his trolley near the ticket machine, and turned to say goodbye.

"Unfortunately," I said, "I have to leave here and take another train going in a different direction. I'm sure you'll be fine. Please enjoy your stay, and again, welcome." I reached out to shake his hand. He took it with both of his, then placed it over his heart and smiled. When he let go, he put both his hands together in namaste, and bowed slightly. I put down my backpack, and returned the gesture.

I gathered my bags and went through the turnstile down to the northbound platform. Once I got there I looked over to the southbound one. A few minutes later I saw an agent leading him along, then help him unload his luggage. He turned and saw me: I waved, he waved back. Then our respective trains came, and we disappeared in opposite directions. I'll be looking for him when I finally get to India.

MUSIC

Studio 2

(2016)

If you're a music fan, you know Studio 2 as a part of the EMI stages in London where the Beatles recorded much of their iconic music. And you also know that EMI changed its name to reflect its location, and is now Abbey Road Studios. However, if you're Lefty, Zeek, Rocky or Smokestack, you know it as Mecca. That's because those are the stage names of The Weeklings, and to call them a Beatles tribute band is missing the point. Sure, they can cover the Fab Four's tunes, note for note. But along with the usual stuff, what they play are Beatles tunes you've never heard unless you are a rabid fan, along with originals that you'd swear were old Lennon-McCartney chestnuts that you just can't place.

In real life, The Weeklings sprang from the friendship and shared sensibilities of Glen Burtnik and Bob Burger. Burtnik (Lefty) was nine when he watched the Beatles on The Ed Sullivan Show: "I wasn't quite sure what I was watching, but it was riveting. Something was definitely happening here. Dad wasn't impressed and my oldest brother Ron thought it was silly. But Ringo got my attention."

Burtnik's fascination with the band led him into music professionally, and in 1978 to portray Paul in "Beatlemania." He started writing songs, built a solo career, and became a well known player in Asbury Park, NJ, part of the local musical fraternity that included Springsteen, Southside Johnny and many others. He toured with Styx and currently plays with The Orchestra, a group which includes former members of ELO. But his Beatles pedigree kept him in the band's musical afterlife, performing at fan fests and conventions. Burtnik and Burger (Zeek) were already playing together, and it was on the circuit they eventually connected with John Merjave (Rocky) and Dave Anthony (Smokestack).

They performed for the first time as The Weeklings at a gig at a library. The audience reaction was such that they thought it was worth pursuing. But it was more than just the Lennon-McCartney-Harrison-Starr sound. Says Burtnik, "We've come to the realization it's not simply about The Beatles. We are inspired by not only them, but a long list of bands in a style some call power pop. It's that combination of rock n roll with melody and harmony and the attitude of the early sixties, when pop bands were exploding."

A year ago they released their first album, containing six original Beatles-inspired tunes, as well as six actual Fab Four tracks that were demos and the like, but had never gotten a proper airing. Reviews were great: "The Weeklings contains 12 tasty slices of melodic bliss that will warm your heart and capture your imagination." And "When an album is as joyous and as entertaining as the debut record from the Weeklings, we feel like shouting our joy from every rooftop around." Another summed it up succinctly: "It doesn't get much better than this."

For the boys, the next move was obvious: for their sophomore effort, they booked that legendary Studio 2. They wrote new tunes, and dug even deeper into the Beatles archives for other stuff never recorded. And on June 8 and 9, in that very same space where musical history was made, they will see if they can conjure up the ghosts of George Martin and his charges. Says Burtnik, "I'm not a kid and I've had much experience recording records in my life. So I don't expect to freeze up or anything. But I'm certain I will be thrilled, standing in the footprints of giants."

Of course, recording doesn't come cheap. And so the band has created a GoFundMe page to enable fans and others help them out. All pledges of support are welcome, with premiums ranging from CD's to house concerts. But sorry: the violin bass that Lefty will use (just like early Paul) has already been claimed.

It isn't often that lighting strikes twice. And Ed Sullivan's not around to invite The Weeklings onto his show. But that's OK. These guys play because 50 years ago a bunch of kids saw and heard something extraordinary on TV, and spent their lives trying to capture it themselves. It started them down a path they have been happily walking ever since. And now it's their turn in that same studio to make their own magic.

Groove, Groove and More Groove

(2011)

Even if you have a tin ear, can't carry a note in a bucket and have all the rhythm that God gave squirrels, back in elementary school you probably had a chance to play the tambourine. It was that round thing nestled on the music teacher's cart between the wooden sticks, the maracas and the cowbell. A double threat, you could bang on it and get a drum sound, or shake it and have it jingle-jangle. In terms of making noise, it made a lot. That's not the same as making music, but it sure could be heard.

And that's probably where you left it. That is, unless you're Julia Joseph. Julia is a wonderful singer-songwriter, named Best Female Jazz Solo Artist in the 2004 New York International Independent Music festival, while her debut CD "Hush" won the 2008 Independent Music Award's popular vote for Best Folk/Singer-Songwriter. She describes her voice as "an alto that has a little crystal or a little grit on the top end." Others go further: Ty Greenstein of the group Girlyman says, "It contains traces of her heroes — Nina Simone, Phoebe Snow, Janis Joplin — but it's more than that," while M. Neala Byrne writes it's "a voice that could awaken the dead and lull the living to sleep."

While her singing and songwriting certainly deserve top billing, Julia also puts her talents to use for others. She works as a session vocalist and back-up singer, and you can hear her on several musical pieces from NBC's hit comedy, "30 Rock." More recently, she has become a permanent support player for fellow singer-songwriter Milton. In each of those roles she brings her voice and her musicality, but also something else: in her own words, she's a "kick-ass tambourine player."

If you see her play, you'd have to agree. Her leads and harmonies certainly add to any performance, but you can't help but notice her tambourine playing. Steady to be sure, it adds to the sound without overpowering it, while also accenting the whole. It's hard to imagine that that little noisemaker can make such a difference. But like many things, in the hands of a skilled practitioner, the ordinary can become extraordinary.

It wasn't always that way. "I took drum lessons a long time ago," she says, "and am happiest when grooving to some kind of rhythm. But for some reason I felt obligated to stick to the 'singer-songwriter' thing." And so guitar became her instrument. But then Milton asked her to join his backup group, and she noticed how integral tambourine and shaker were to many of the tracks. "So I lied and told him I could handle all that stuff in the live shows and that I was a 'real' player." But then she had to pony up: "At our first rehearsal, I was a little late because I had to run and buy a tambourine. I threw the packaging away outside the rehearsal room, walked in and winged it. No one was the wiser." She eventually came clean, but a "player" was born.

Now the owner of 6 different varieties, she approaches her playing as would any other musician. "You need to be very good at dividing beats evenly and with good dynamic emphasis. That's how you make it groove! When a rhythm section is locked in and tight, the music lives." Put another way, "It's an instrument. It makes sound. A LOT of sound. If you're going to play one, play it for real, or every drummer you work with is just really going to hate you."

I asked her if there are tambourine players she admires. "Jack Ashford... is the guy responsible for the back-beat in the 'Motown Sound.' He played tambourine on everything, and if you really listen you can hear how much that tambourine is making the sound. Rosalie "Lady Tambourine" Washington is also truly something to behold. She is legendary for sitting in with the big acts who perform at the New Orleans Jazz Festival." Julia gets the possibilities: "Do not be fooled by how simple it looks or seems! There's all kinds of craziness a master can do. I mean, imagine a truly gripping tambourine solo? They do exist! I can't do one yet, no way... but it sure is a satisfying idea."

Just how important is her playing as opposed to her singing? "To me it's just a different part of the music. It's part of what's driving the rhythm. I guess if anything I was doing wasn't important, it would be nixed." Decide for yourself. Catch her live, and hear her singing and writing ability. Catch her with Milton, and watch her mastery of the tambourine. Or in her words, watch her add, "Dynamic, dimension, groove, groove and more groove."

Let the Girls Play

(2014)

First the disclaimer: I live in the Northeast, so anything I write about country music is suspect at best. Like guns and NASCAR, the fact the certain things have overwhelming followings in areas outside of the Boston-New York-Washington corridor that aren't based on Yankee sensibilities seems, frankly, unbelievable. But yes, to those of us to whom brunch in Red Hook is considered the height of cool, there are places where Luke Bryan is at least as well-known as Jay-Z, where Florida Georgia Line isn't a border between two states but a group with whose song "Cruise" dominated the charts with 20 weeks in the top spot.

It's a genre that was written off as "mature" not too long ago, described by one music critic as "stoic men in ten-gallon hats and soprano women who'd lived full lives singing songs about, divorce, war, and that aching, hollow heartbreak feeling." No more. Fusing elements of rap and pop to its country roots, it's moved far beyond Johnny Cash and Ernest Tubbs and Patsy Cline to Jason Aldean and Brantley Gilbert and Chase Rice. You can argue about the definition, and just how heir-to-the-throne-of-George-Strait these new comers really are, but this is most definitely NOT your daddy's country. Put another way, if you know the former three and not the later, they you don't really have you finger on the right pulse point.

But while that body may have a lot of blood pumping through it in the form of airplay, there's a problem: it's mostly male. With Taylor Swift no longer considered a country girl, the charts are dominated as almost never before by men. And not just any kind of men, but young, fit, hard partying types singing about the three "b's," usually explained as some combination of babes, bars and beers. In the so-called "bro-country" movement, every night is a Friday Night, every vehicle is a truck and every girl is lit by moonlight, has painted-on jeans and loves to drink Bud.

While there's some sense that this particular pickup is running out of steam, some are trying a little harder to, if not push the vehicle into a ditch, at least let some others share the road. And that means not just songs that appeal to a more female sensibility, but performers on that side of the ledger as well. And it's the idea behind a rotating group of female singer-songwriters known collectively as the Song Suffragettes.

With the slogan "Let the Girls Play," the idea was hatched back in March by music industry veteran Todd Cassetty and Helena Capps as a way of encouraging more female artists. Having outgrown their first home in Nashville, they now convene every

Monday night at the Listening Room Café on Second Avenue South. Since they started, over 60 different young ladies have taken the stage, some well-known only in their home towns, others veterans of shows like "The Voice" and "American Idol," but all showcasing their very considerable songwriting and performing chops.

On a stage backed by white damask curtains, fronted by a few old lamps and some mismatched chairs, the format is simple. Each of the five or so performers introduces herself, and plays and sings one of her own songs. They go down the line, circle back to do it again, then perform a group cover of a more well-known tune. The night I visited a solid and appreciative audience heard Betsy Lane do "Southern Crazy" while Kalie Shorr sang "God Sees Everything," each a hit waiting to be discovered or perhaps recorded by a more well-known name. There were equally good offerings from Daisy Mallory, Karli Chayne and Gracie Schram. And not one mentioned a pickup truck.

The music business is a fickle one. Talent and determination are table stakes at best, assuring nothing other than a chance to perform for your family and friends and perhaps a few interested strangers who might buy a CD. Anyone can do that. But making even a bare-bones a living at it? That's a different story. And becoming the next Reba McEntire or Miranda Lambert or Faith Hill? That's not a story, it's a fairy tale. But regardless of the eventual outcome, the first step is to play and be heard. And that's what Song Suffragettes is all about. Let the girls play. You just might like what you hear.

Not So Simple Men

(2018)

In terms of music videos, "Exit 49" follows a relatively straightforward storyline that's part of the canon. The band portrays a bunch of office workers chafing under an oppressive boss. They revolt and break free, with the boss giving chase. They run to their instruments and play, with the music driving the guy back as he confronts them. There's slo-mo, quick cuts and lots of closeups of the band. Been there, done that.

Then again, there are some unique touches. The boss is a surrealistic puppet with a snake coming out of his forehead. The band runs to the beach, where the puppet chases them in the sand, eventually levitating above them. And the lead singer is an orthodox Jew with a yarmulke, sideburns and a prayer shawl. So yeah, there is that.

None of this would be more than a weird curiosity if the music weren't so good. It's a polished and listenable blend of rap, folk, rock and indie, underlying a perceptive and well written lyric. The more you listen to it the more it starts to grow on you. In an intentional bit of irony, the band is called Simple Man, though it's anything but.

The least simple of the men in the band is singer, songwriter and lead vocalist, Yaakov Kafka. He says he was into rap as long as he could remember, predating his embrace of an observant lifestyle and orthodox practice. As a teenager and young adult, he wrote and recorded several songs where he grew up in New Jersey. Moving to Israel to explore his religious roots and spirituality, he kept writing and recording. While there he started collaborating with acoustic guitarist Tamir Tusia, who grew up in Israel and also became observant as a young adult. Returning to these shores, they crossed paths with Eli Weiss, another orthodox Jew and electric guitar player who counts BB King as an influence.

But while their faith informs their music it doesn't define it. And so needing some bottom for their sound they got connected with bassist Clayton McIntyre. Known as "Church" for where he played a lot, the Jamaican came from a different set of religious and cultural traditions. Add in drummer Pat Mooney, an Irish Catholic with a taste for soul, and you have a true musical melting pot. In fact, when the band sends out its samplers for gigs and airplay, they describe their music as "Genre-Confused."

And that it is, though extremely listenable. There's a dash of Kendrick Lamar, a touch of the Lumineers, mixed with the soul of Nick Hakim and a splash of Al Green. If you inhale really deeply you can detect whiffs of trance and jazz and more. Or as my son said when I played it for him, "Not ANOTHER mixed-race orthodox acoustic alterna-rap group!?" But somehow it just works.

As for the songs, they reflect the fact that the bandmates are older, more spiritual than they were as kids. They're not trying to preach, but they do have something to say. As Yaakov says, "In an increasingly divisive world, we feel like there is something meaningful, in both the composition of the band and message we have." Musically and lyrically they're steeped in the styles on which they grew up, though filtered through a more adult sensibility. Or as Clayton put it, "the music has to be something I'm proud of, something I can play for my son." Yaakov puts it this way: "Who am I doing this for, is it just for the moment, or is it something more?"

What do they hope to get out of this? Well, they're not giving up their day jobs just yet. But if they can push it beyond a few hundred "likes," beyond family and friends, that would be great. Yaakov again: "A lot of our lyrics are connected to internal struggles and conflict, about being pulled in different directions, about trying to make sense of the world and find our own true voice. If people can relate to that, and our music inspires them to fully inhabit their own lives and selves, that would give us the greatest satisfaction. We want the music to be the escape, but the message isn't escapism." Or as the chorus goes in "Exit 49," "We're leaving now to see the sounds. Peace, we out."

STUFF

Saved By The Bud

(2017)

Paul and I went inside to place the order. We were midway through our wait for an outside table and had already killed a bottle of wine, a dozen oysters, some shrimp and some fried calamari. It was no problem: the rain and had passed, and it had turned into a nice night. And so having appetizers and some drinks while sitting on the restaurant's patio, chatting and watching the boats go by wasn't exactly rough duty.

But horrors, we realized our bottle of wine was empty. With the place being busy, we decided to head in to the bar and get another ourselves, rather than waiting for a waitress to come to us. We ordered, then both reached for our wallets and started to argue over who would pay. The busy bartender let us go for a few seconds, then had had enough: "Why don't I just split it for you?" We agreed, and he grabbed our cards and turned away. He quickly came back with a new bottle and sales slips. We each scribbled our names, grabbed the cards and the wine, and headed back outside to our wives.

In short order our table was called and we sat down. We enjoyed the food, the view, the remaining wine and the company.

When the check came, I grabbed it. After all, Paul and his wife had been most generous in inviting us to their place by the beach for the weekend, and had even gotten the first round of drinks. The least we could do was buy them dinner, and we were still not even-steven. We departed and headed back to their place for the night.

The next morning we all awoke and decided to go to a local spot for breakfast. Once again I picked up the check, feeling that barely equaled their hospitality. Afterwards we headed back to their place, then to the beach for a bit before needing to start for home. They said they were going to do some errands before going back themselves. And so we thanked them and headed out, stopping for gas before we got on the highway.

It was later on Monday when my phone rang with Paul's number. I was wondering if we accidentally left something behind, or maybe took something we shouldn't have. It was neither and both at the same time. Turns out that that day they were also having company, just back in the city. Their nephew was coming for dinner, and so Paul had gone out to get the fixin's. He got spaghetti, ground meat and some salad stuff. For good measure, he threw a six-pack of beer in the cart. When he got to the checkout lane, it got rung up no problem. Until it came to the beer.

Paul's a youthful looking guy, but there is little doubt that he's old enough to drink. Still, a "we card everybody" policy is still a policy, even when you're confronted with a customer that looks closer to Social Security than college. And so Paul pulled out his license to prove that this Bud was for him. Except it wasn't. Because while the license identified him as him, the credit card identified him as me.

In best CSI fashion, we figured it must have happened when the bartender split the tab for the bottle of wine. We both have Chase Sapphire credit cards, which are dark blue with the name embossed in gold. Frankly, they are hard to read in good light, let alone in a busy bar after a bottle of wine. I guess when we got the cards back from the barkeep, we didn't notice the swap.

And so I happily used his going forward from that time. That dinner we bought them? On his card. The breakfast we also treated them to? Same. Even that tank of gas to get us home? Turns out it was all courtesy of our hosts for the weekend. And all he got to put on my card was some pasta and meatballs.

So forget passwords. Forget special three-digit verification codes. None of it stopped us from using another's card. In fact, had it not been for the six-pack and a by-the-book checker, we could have gone to Europe this month on Paul. Damn you, Budweiser.

Gunk n' Stuff

(2012)

It seems as though virtually every ad, every article, every product that counts itself as contemporary carries the word "digital" as the two jacks just to get into the game. The library has digital books. You can shoot digital photographs. Your car has digital gauges. There are digital ovens, digital toys, digital vacuum cleaners. And yes, there are even digital gloves, offering the digital experience to your digits.

But what does any of that mean? In its purest sense, digital means the data involved is discontinuous. That is, it makes individual, discrete steps from one thing to another. That's as opposed to the way the world really is, an analog state of affairs. More simply, things are continuous as opposed to this or that, tall or short, blue or red. Forget 50 shades of gray: there are a zillion. And to be really accurate, there are an infinite amount: you can always slide a little one way or the other to something else more illegal, more immoral or more fattening.

Still, we have come to expect that digital is how we manage the world. Partly that's because it's how computers work: they reduce everything to ones and zeros. Partly because it gives us faith that broken things can be fixed: it either works or it doesn't. And partly because it helps to provide explanations for the unknowable: if they bombard enough particles at that collider in Switzerland, sooner or later we will get a digital picture of another that shows how things work, though it's still all mumbo-jumbo no matter how many cute animations they trot out.

And yet things aren't that neat. No matter how hard we try, you can't always reduce things down to a simple yes or no. Certainly we see that in the current political environment. For while absolutes make for great campaign slogans ("No new taxes!" "The fault is with the banks!"), they don't recognize the reality of on the ground. Most issues and explanations bear a more nuanced approach, an analog one if you will. And while it may not be as comforting, it is more in line with the real world.

The best example comes recently from American Airlines. On three different flights over the past few weeks, seats came loose while planes were in the air. We're not talking a broken armrest or tray table. We're talking about whole rows that suddenly tilted back. Forget fasten your seat belt: how about fasten your seat.

While there was some initial speculation that the problem might be tied to lax maintenance in light of labor troubles, by all accounts it's purely a mechanical issue related to cabin remodeling.

Still, when pressed to explain the cause of the problem, there was no digital answer. That would have been something like "The R7/S33 opine clamping mechanism was installed incorrectly" or "Upon inspection, the Z81Alpha retaining bolt had a crack in it" or "We've had a failure of the 74G-22 Hyper-rigid frimit." Any of those explanations, while disturbing, would have been acceptable. Something is broken, let's identify it, let's fix it.

But according to airline spokeswoman Mary Frances Fagan, the seat lock plunger mechanism got "gunked up over time with people spilling sodas, popcorn, coffee or whatever." Gunk. Is there anything more analog than that? While she may have mentioned the component elements involved, I doubt they have a chemical formula for it. Then again, maybe they do: a product called "Fudge Urban De-Gunk Deep Clean Shampoo" promises to "remove the excess product build up that can leave your hair looking dull and oily!" As a frequent flier, if a bottle of shampoo is what it takes to keep a 757 in the air, so be it.

Still, it is refreshing to acknowledge that things are indeed analog and sometimes mushy. We even saw it in the Vice Presidential debate. You can like or hate Joe Biden, but when he tried to dismiss Paul Ryan's charges and defend the sanctions against Iran, the exchange took a colorful turn. "This is a bunch of stuff," Biden said. "What does that mean?" asked moderator

Martha Raddatz. "It's Irish," Ryan said. "We Irish call it malarkey," chimed in Biden.

Stuff and gunk. Makes one wonder: it may be green, but is gunk Irish too? Now, there's something we could use the super collider to figure out.

I'm With Tim

(2015)

By his own admission, one of the candidates for president is building his campaign by harnessing grass roots momentum as opposed to counting on support from any major party. His policy positions are more broadly thematic rather than specific, focusing on world peace, fiscal restraint and smaller government. And he views his business background as one of his strongest qualifications, believing that his skills in that arena are exactly what are needed for the nation's chief executive. Unlike Donald Trump, however, his views on women are a good bit softer. As he and I stood talking and my wife walked up, he looked at me, then looked at her, and said with a smile, "Well, she makes you look good!"

Meet Tim Farkas, full time candidate for President of the United States.

Farkas was in the sub-prime mortgage business in his native Ohio, and has had some legal and business issues. But just like that other businessman in the race, he hardly sees that as a disqualifier. Quite the opposite: "I used to run a company with about 200 people, give or take, that all worked on commission. And when someone can get 200 people to work on a commission-only basis, then they understand how hard it is to get things done. So I think I have some good ideas and recommendations to get the right people around me and do the right things."

But to get elected you have to court the voters, and Farkas goes about it the old fashioned way. When I met him he was standing on the corner of 42nd and Sixth Avenue in New York City, the same way he stands on streets in his hometown of Columbus. He had a hand-written sign propped up on a table, and a stack of business cards in his hand. He made a beeline for every person walking by, offering them a card and telling them "It's your country. If you have something you want to say, drop it in my mailbox." Then on to the next. Since I was just standing there waiting for my wife, we got to talking.

He began by pointing out the many challenges we face as a country, specifically focusing on the national debt. "I know guys who are really good at finance," he told me. Beyond that? "It's a big problem," he said. Yup, I didn't disagree. "Lots of people have good ideas, and we need to use them." Hard to argue with that as well. "We have the freedom to believe. The United States of America gives us the freedom to believe." I agreed it was indeed a great country, but we had issues. He nodded, and threw out what is sort of his campaign slogan: "We need to get our country back." Perhaps not as pithy as Ben Carson's "Heal. Inspire. Revive." but certainly not as clunky as Rand Paul's "Defeat The Washington Machine. Unleash The American Dream," even if that one does rhyme.

It was about at this point that my wife walked up. She saw me standing there talking to a guy with a scruffy beard in shorts and shoes with no socks, and probably assumed I had had bumped into an old friend. I introduced her to him with a line I don't get to use everyday: "This is Tim. He's running for President of the United States." She smiled at me and cocked her head, with a look that asked is he dangerous, crazy or just curious, and regardless, why in heaven's name was I standing there talking to him? Then he complimented her, and we all laughed. I shook hands with him, wished him luck and started to head to dinner. As we walked away, he handed me a card, and closed with his signature request and offer: "If you have something you want to put on my website, drop me a line."

Including Farkas, there are 24 declared candidates for the highest office in the land. There are sitting governors and senators, ex's of both stripes, and successful professionals from outside of politics, all trying to distinguish themselves from the pack. In that light, I would bet that Tim is likely the only one you'll meet standing on the street asking you to give him a call. In this hyper competitive race, maybe the others should take notice.

Internet Sensation

(2017)

Let me be very clear: this is not about me.

Yes, I have an assortment of social media accounts. But I readily admit that I'm more a stalker than a poster. Other than this column, I don't put up anything. Mind you, I'm not casting aspersions on those that do. I just prefer to live my life a little quieter. If I'm being honest, I don't think that 95% of what I do is interesting to anyone besides my immediate family. And even then I'm not so sure.

Still, I do admit to occasionally scanning Facebook and Twitter and the like. I enjoy seeing some of the kid shots, some of the sassy comments, some of the new ventures in which people are involved. But it's hardly a regular thing. Yes, I'm sure I'm missing the latest cute cat picture, but it's a sacrifice with which I've made peace.

That helps to explain why I was ignorant to what I was happening around me. I was at the NBA All Star Game in New Orleans munching popcorn when three people sat down behind me. They looked like regular fans - a mom, dad and an older college-aged kid. Other than the fact that the woman had on a rather ugly sweater with "NBA Champs" on it, nothing made them stand out. I smiled and said hello, and turned back to the action on the floor. But while I wasn't really paying attention, I sensed a few people around me mildly excited by their presence. Indeed, some even got up and came over with comments like "I recognize that sweater. Are you really her? I love you! Can I get a picture?" They grabbed a selfie and went back to their seats. I began to wonder: who was "her?"

The game started, and I noted the three wildly applauding Steph Curry and Klay Thompson, two All Stars from the Golden State Warriors. I turned and asked if they too were from California. The son nodded and indicated his tee shirt, which had a Golden State logo on it. At the same time a person wearing official looking NBA credentials came over and had a quick conversation, checking on their seats, seeing how they were faring and thanking them for coming. None of that answered who she was, though she was obviously someone.

A few minutes later another NBA staffer came over, this one with a headset. He introduced himself to "Robin" and started to explain the drill. "You ready?" he began. Robin nodded. "So at the next timeout, here's how it will go. On the screen we'll do a 'Wheel of Fortune' kind of thing. The first will be a robot cam, then a kiss cam. Next will be the Dancing Mom cam. We'll take 2 other random moms, then come to you. You should start, but keep going after they go on to the next. The announcer will suddenly realize it was you, and we'll come back. Then it's all yours. Any questions?" Robin indicated she understood completely.

Still not sure what I was sitting in front of, I realized that if she was going to be on camera, I would be that hapless guy in the foreground wondering what was happening behind him. I jumped up and sat down on the stairs across from my seat. I apologized to the guy I was crowding, but he was beaming watching Robin as well. So I asked him: who was she? Thankfully he knew it all. Robin Schreiber was a 60-ish retired school teacher and a 28-year season ticket holder who became an internet sensation when she jumped up to dance when the camera picked her up at a game in November (Search "Dance Cam Mom"). Since then, she has danced with the Warriors' cheerleaders at center court, Steph Curry and even Coach Steve Kerr. And she was about to do it again for the entire arena.

Sure enough, it went down just as described. First the people doing the robot, then a few kisses, then some other dancing moms, all to the audience's mild amusement. Then they came to Robin. She jumped up and started, and the place went wild. If you watch you'll see her patented hip pump, her hand waves and her arm flares. You'll see the people round her applauding and taking pics. But the best part?

You won't see me.

Seniored

(2016)

There were a number of factors that could have been in play. I was in a major southern city, where manners and "yes ma'am" are still part of the territory. It was before official opening time at the mall, so the only people around were workers getting the place ready for the day and early morning walkers, most of whom tend to be older. And it was a cold and rainy morning, so I was wearing a heavy jacket and carrying a dripping umbrella. Yes, I looked bedraggled.

While I don't usually go shopping in malls either at home or on the road, I had wandered over from my hotel in the quest to fill an hour before I had to leave for the airport. Arriving 20 minutes before the stores themselves opened, I headed to the food court to get a cup of coffee and sit for a few minutes to check messages before taking a stroll. Wanting something more substantial that what was offered at the ubiquitous Starbucks, I headed to a popular chain that had a morning menu.

In spite of the saturation marketing that seems to be everywhere, I confess to not being up to speed on all the combinations and permutations of franchise breakfast food. There are combinations, package deals and cutely named offerings that require a spreadsheet to fully understand. I mean, what's a King Croissan'wich, and how does it differ from a Sausage McGriddle? And so I stood there studying the menu for a few moments, trying to figure out what to order.

The young lady at the counter gave me a minute, then asked me what I wanted. I started with what I knew: "Bacon egg and cheese, please." She asked me how I wanted it on: on a muffin, a biscuit or a roll. I thought for a moment, and went with the muffin. Anything else she said. "Coffee, please" I said. Done and done.

As I watched her enter my order, I caught the display on the terminal out of the corner of my eye. She was fast, so fast that I almost missed the fact that two letters popped up on the screen in front of the word "coffee" before the total cost appeared. They didn't register, but I know I saw them. She stepped away to put my sandwich in a bag and pour me a cup of joe. She threw in some creamers and napkins, pointed to where the sugar was located, and took the emerging receipt from the slot and handed it to me. As I walked away, I looked at it. In front of the coffee were the letters "SR."

For the first time in my life, I had been seniored.

For the record, I am still on the low side of 60. True, what hair I do have has more than its share of gray, and my face shows a few traces of, shall we say, my years of experience. So in spite of what I like to think of as my youthful countenance, I could easily understand how the woman behind the counter looked up half an hour before anything was open to see an older man standing in front of her. He was staring at the menu wearing a wet leather coat, carrying a dripping umbrella, pondering what the "kids" are eating today. I, too, would have made the assumption that his social security check was likely in the mail.

I put my food down on an empty table (in fact, at the hour they were all empty) then circled back to the counter. No customers were there, and the young lady was in back putting something away. I waited until she came back, then approached her. I smiled: "I'm not mad, and I don't really care, but can you tell me what that means?" I said, pointing to the "SR" on the receipt. She looked at it, then me: "That's senior coffee," she said. "Well," I asked, "just how hold do you think I am?" She looked at me, and hesitated a bit, not sure what she should say. "I don't really know," she started, "but, well, it's cheaper that way." I laughed, thanked her, then headed back to my table. I guess it's begun. And while it's not like I want to belong to the club, if it saved me 50 cents, well, I guess I'm OK with that.

To Seal or Not To Seal

(2017)

I have scoured the web sites of home and kitchen doyens like Martha and Rachel. I have checked out the literature posted by the FDA, the CDC and an alphabet soup of other agencies. I have Googled and Safaried and Firefoxed endlessly through the views of self-proclaimed experts with handles like FreshGuy and SafetySal. And while I find opinions, musings, ramblings, cautionary tales, anecdotes, admonitions and more, I can find no definitive information one way or the other.

The conundrum goes like this. Open up a new container of some foodstuff, and when you take off the topmost closure you will find another one underneath. It might be foil or some kind of stiff paper or a type of plastic. These generally serve one of two functions, and sometimes both. The first is as a safety seal. Ever since the Tylenol incident in the 1980's where bottles of painkiller were laced with cyanide, killing a number of people, manufacturers have used these to guarantee the purity of their product. The second function is to maintain the freshness of the product. Doesn't matter if it's cottage cheese or vitamins, the only way to insure that the stuff inside makes it from the manufacturing plant to your house still creamy or potent is to stop air from getting in. And that's where the seal comes in.

In the first case, once you break it, the jig is up. One and done, the telltale has done its job, proving that you were first and only user. Feel free to dig into that jar of coffee or tub of crumbled feta cheese and enjoy with abandon. You can consume the contents knowing that no one was there before you (or at least since it has left the factory).

And since its mission here on this green earth has been fulfilled, you can most assuredly get rid of the detritus. Whether it comes off as a single piece, or you have to tear it out bit by bit like old flocked wallpaper that's been there for 20 years (sorry, homeowner flashback), it has no need to exist anymore. All it's doing is getting in your way when you go back for a second helping. Unless you want to be use it as some sort of, say, single peanut dispenser as a way of limiting your legume intake, just rip that sucker off like a Band-Aid.

But in the second instance, while the seal has served a useful function up to the moment you open the product, what then? Here's where the research is sketchy at best. Common sense would seem to say that once you let the air into the can or jar or tub or whatever, the damage has been done. From then on it's only a matter of time until all that icky stuff floating in the air takes hold and that cottage cheese goes from pearly white to slimy green.

And yet many carefully peel the seal up on one side, and smooth it back over the cream cheese or margarine when done before replacing the outer cover. They feel that it helps to keeps the contents fresher, or at the very least, makes the outer lid fit tighter. It might not be a Tupperware or Zip-Loc level barrier, but the logic is that that little extra bit of snugness will keep the cream cheese creamier longer.

There are strong feelings on both sides. Similar to debates as to which is the correct way to hang toilet paper, it has a lot to do with what your folks did when you were a kid. And devotees on both sides are passionate about their positions and reasons. Add this to gun control, abortion rights and school prayer as an area where we are divided as a nation.

So in that spirit, while I doubt I will change any minds, here's what I've gleaned from my surfing. 1) Once you break the seal, the damage is done. Air is part of the equation, and no good can come from that. Take it off. 2) By keeping the plastic on, you might actually be making it worse, as every time you have to peel it back you are touching it, introducing another possible source of contamination. 3) If we're talking Pringles, just eat the whole damn can at one sitting, and then there's no issue.

More Understandable-er

(2018)

In his book "Thing Explainer," Randall Monroe endeavors to describe and explain the inner workings of complex stuff using line drawings and a vocabulary of the 1000 most common words. As the creator of the web comic "xkcd" and a guy with a BS in Physics, his qualifications and sensibility make him the obvious heir to the work of David Macaulay, whose "The Way Things Work" did the same thing 30 years ago. Using just "ten hundred" words, Monroe reduces things to their most basic elements, starting with the table of contents ("Things in the Book by Page") thru the forward ("Page Before the Book Starts") and on to things like elevators ("Lifting Rooms") and dishwashers ("Box That Cleans Food Holders").

Monroe came to mind because of an article about China's development of a rail hub in Eastern Europe. As part of its "One Belt, One Road" program to extend its reach for trade, that country has been buying seaports around the world to increase its footprint. But in this case there is no water anywhere even close to the tracks. Indeed, the hub in Khorgos, Kazakhstan is about as far from the sea as you can get. And – here's where Monroe's expertise at simplification might have been helpful – that particular point has an actual name: the Pole of Inaccessibility.

Not a babka baker named Wojciech who lives in Krakow and doesn't like to talk to anyone, there are actually eight Poles of Inaccessibility in the world, one on each land mass as well as in the Pacific Ocean. In practice they are generally the most remote places you can be: in the outback in Australia, or in North Dakota in the US to name two. In geographical terms, they are often defined as the furthest location from the coastlines of a continent. In short, if you want to get any from it all, these may actually be the spots.

But in a 140-character world, that moniker is a bit much. It echoes the best (or worst, depending on your point of view) of German linguistic inventions. That language is well known for combining simple words into complex ones that result in a new construct. For example, in English we might describe a guy as the captain of a steamship that plies the Danube. But in the Fatherland that has a very specific word of its own: Donaudampfschiffahrtsgesellschaftskapitän. I'll leave it to speakers of that mother tongue to puzzle out the feminine version.

That's not to say that on these shores there aren't examples where we have slang standing in for official terms. Certain fields have highly technical descriptions that we mere mortals have reduced to their essence. A doctor might tell you to drink water if you have synchronous diaphragmatic flutter, which is the medical description for the hiccups. Likewise, if your physician tells you that that pain in your head is sphenopalatine ganglioneuralgia, you might be think you were going to die. Not to worry: that's the correct term for an ice cream headache.

The corollary are those compact words or phrases that describe complex actions. You see these perhaps most notably in sports. In baseball if a pitcher aborts his throw after he's started it, we call that a balk. In football, a long throw down the field with little chance of success is a Hail Mary. In tennis, lose a set without winning a game and you've been bageled. And in cricket, if a bowler who would normally spin the ball toward a right-handed batsman spins it away from him, that's a doosra. Reverse it, and it's a googly.

But back to our geography lesson. There's nothing in the phrase in question that's meant to be ironic or flip. (That stands in contrast to Colin Bateman's book about a hard-drinking bicycle-riding journalist in Northern Ireland, titled after the vehicle that gets him from fight to fight: "Cycle of Violence.") Still, while Pole of Inaccessibility may be technically correct, it's a mouthful that takes mental time to decode. So perhaps going forward, it might be worth taking a page from Randall Monroe's book, and strip it down to its simplest components. In that light, might I suggest "most far away-est place" as a substitute. And that way when you mention the Pole of Inaccessibility, you WILL be talking about that babka baker in Krakow named Wojciech.

Count Steps or Else

(2017)

It's one of the great names in one of the best bad movies of our time: Snake Plisken in "Escape from New York." If you don't know the 1981 film, it takes place in a then distant 1997, when the President's plane crashes into a Manhattan which has been turned into a maximum security prison controlled by violent gangs. Kurt Russell, as Snake, a "scruffy, one-eyed, famous special-forces-soldier-turned-convicted-armed-robber," is tasked with rescuing him in exchange for a pardon. As an extra added incentive, Plisken is injected with an explosive device that will only be defused if he completes the task. It's not too much of a spoiler to say he succeeds and lives, and is so successful that he is tasked several years later with rescuing the President's daughter from a similar hell in "Escape from LA" or he will not be given the antidote to the virus with which he was infected that time. Thankfully, the fictional president's family was not as large as the size of current occupant of the White House, or Plisken would still be making milk runs.

And what brings this current random bit of movie nostalgia to mind? It's the tale of Dina Mitchell and her activity tracker. Next to smartphones, activity trackers, of which Fitbit is the most ubiquitous, have become the must-have electronic accessory of the moment. At their simplest they have an accelerometer and so are able to measure movement, which they display as steps. The more advanced models can also record vertical changes as in climbing stairs, and even your sleep patterns. For most, the reports they offer are a mere curiosity, good as a gentle form of encouragement, coaching and prodding to get you up off the couch. Others are so obsessed with the readouts that you'd think they were training for the Olympics, and need to know their pulse-oxygen ratio at any given moment.

Still, few would argue that any movement is good movement, and if making the little flower bloom on the face of the device by hitting your target step count does it for you, then go for it. After all, what's the worst that could happen? The flower doesn't grow, that's all. Wake up the next day, and the whole thing resets and you go again. Even if you sync it with your computer, and you've linked it to a support group, it's not like you will be getting hate texts from your pals excoriating you for falling short of your goal. Odds of a Jeff Sessions-like public tweet-shaming are pretty low.

Which brings us back to Dina. Mitchell was a Fitbit user, and wore a Flex 2, given to her a few weeks before as a birthday present. Little is reported about her personal habits, whether she was a casual user or a serious physical fitness aficionado. What is known is that she was sitting quietly and reading a book when the device strapped to her wrist "exploded." She went to a local urgent care facility, where doctors removed small pieces of rubber and plastic from her arm left by the melting device, leaving behind second degree burns.

Fitbit said they were investigating the issue and issued a statement: "We are extremely concerned about Ms. Mitchell's report regarding her Flex 2 and take it very seriously, as the health and safety of our customers is our top priority." They said they have had no other reports similar to this, see no reason for people to stop wearing their Flex 2's, and offered Dina a new device to replace her old one.

You can look at this two ways. Taken at face value, it is a random accident to a poor woman, and it ends there. Nothing more. Or what they're NOT telling us is that this was a next generation device that they were field testing surreptitiously. In that scenario, it goes something like this: Dina's step count was low. Dina should have been up and moving. Dina decided that rather than go to the gym, she would sit in a comfy chair and read a book. Not on my watch, said the Flex 2. And BOOM! Just a little behavioral conditioning. You gotta believe that the next time Dina has a choice between getting on the treadmill, or sitting down and paging through Vogue, she'll think twice.

Just remember what could have happened to Snake.

Name Changer

(2014)

Consider the predicament of Matt Broomfield and Peter Endicott of London, the editors of the student magazine at Oxford University. Or Jim Fleshman from the Cameron Park Zoo in Waco TX, the Chairman of the Board of Trustees for the International Species Information System. Likewise Dr. Herbert Bernstein from Hampshire College in Amherst, MA, the President & Chief Scientist of the Institute for Science and Interdisciplinary Studies. Each of them probably envies Mayor Lorraine Pyefinch in Queensland, Australia. You see, back in 2008, Mayor Pyefinch and her constituents dodged a bullet when they redrew the local governance lines. That's when their name changed to its current incarnation of the Bundaberg Region. Before that, had you journeyed down under, you would have had to call it by its former name, one that is shared not only by the aforementioned groups, but with one entity more in the news these days. For that area of Queensland was formerly known as the Shire of Isis.

While you can pin a lot of things on Australia, being the home of today's most notorious terrorist group is not one of them. The current ISIS, or "Islamic State of Iraq and Syria," has grown from an offshoot of al-Qaeda to a self-declared Caliphate straddling the border between those two troubled countries. The group has become known for their extreme ideology and brutality, and taken the name of the Egyptian goddess of fertility to places it was never intended. That's not to say it hadn't gotten a workout before this. After all, it is also the name of a pharmaceutical developer, a line of lingerie from the British company Ann Summers and a post-metal rock band whose 2009 album "Wavering Radiant" on the Ipecac label opened with the well-received "Hall of the Dead."

Then there's Verizon. Back in 2010 the communications giant and its partners were looking for a moniker to differentiate their new mobile payment venture from PayPal and Google. I'm sure when they tallied up all the focus group responses and marketing research, ISIS Mobile seemed like a clear winner. But odds are better than even that their branding gurus are having second, third and even fourth thoughts right about now.

After all, aside from the difficulty of creating a marketing message ("Triumph with ISIS" or something similar), there are some practical issues as well. Any web search for ISIS results not in connections to the platform, its mobile apps and all the great advantages it has over its competitors, but to images of marauding thugs in black hoods. Sure you can find links to ISIS Wallet, but they are three pages in. And oh, about that web page. The one the company registered is PayWithIsis.com. Since exchanging money with terrorist organizations is a federal offense, people might not rush to buy their potholders from Etsy using the platform. As Michael Abbott, CEO of Isis Mobile said in a statement, "As a company, we have made the decision to rebrand." Good call, that.

But it might not be necessary. Officials and the media have tried several nom de guerres to see what resonates with the public. And in fact, in recognition of the group's larger ambitions, both the U.N. and the U.S. State Department have recently been referring to ISIS as ISIL. That stands for "Islamic State of Iraq and the Levant," where Levant is a broader term for the region, encompassing not just Syria, but Turkey as well as other countries. In that light, Verizon and the others might wind up in the clear after all is said and done. But in a case of one man's ceiling being another man's floor, one can only imagine the anguished conversations among the attendees last week at the annual convention of the right-leaning Libertarian group the "International Society for Individual Liberty." After all, their initials are – well - you can figure it out.

If there's good news, I guess it's that either abbreviation is as lightly used and known as it is. Imagine the gnashing of teeth, sleepless nights and endless meetings that would ensue if they had taken the name "Waji Hali Monafa' Lana IllHeta Iradicali'." A rough translation of that Arabic is the "Front for the Organization of the

Radical Divine." In that light, "Built FORD Tough" takes on a whole new meaning, doesn't it?

ABOUT THE AUTHOR

Marc Wollin is a writer, producer, director and stage manager for video and live events. His column Glancing Askance has been published since 1995, reaches over 10,000 readers on a weekly basis and has been named the Best Humor Column in its class by the New York Press Association.

He lives in Bedford NY with his wife Susan.

Online at

https://glancingaskance.blogspot.com

ALSO BY MARC WOLLIN

Glancing Askance:
Essays on People and Food and Stuff

Glancing Askance
More Essays on People and Food and Stuff